KNOWLEDGE IS POWER
BRADFORD MECHANICS INSTITUTE
No. 7198
Class No.
May be kept
14 Days

FIRST FINDS

A Yorkshire Childhood

Also by June Barraclough

The Heart of the Rose (Weidenfeld & Nicolson 1985)
Rooks Nest (Weidenfeld & Nicolson 1986)
Kindred Spirits (Severn House 1988)
A Time To Love (Methuen 1989)
Generations (Heinemann 1990)
Time Will Tell (Robert Hale 1992)
Familiar Acts (Robert Hale 1993)
Portrait of Maud (Severn House 1994)
Swifter Wings Than Time (Robert Hale 1994)
Ghosts At Cockrow (Janus Publishing Co. 1994)
Daughter of Haworth (Robert Hale 1995)
Family Snapshots (Robert Hale 1995)
No Time Like The Present (Robert Hale 1997)
The Villa Violetta (Robert Hale 1997)

Translation:
Condorcet: Esquisse d'un tableau historique du progrès
de l'esprit humain (Weidenfeld and Nicolson 1955)

Writing as June Benn:
The Woman's View, an anthology (Routledge 1967)

Memorials: an anthology for Funerals and Memorial Services
(Ravette 1986)

FIRST FINDS

A Yorkshire Childhood

June Barraclough

JANUS PUBLISHING COMPANY
London, England

First published in Great Britain 1998
by Janus Publishing Company Limited,
Edinburgh House, 19 Nassau Street,
London W1N 7RE

www.januspublishing.co.uk

**A CIP catalogue record for this book
is available from the British Library.**

ISBN 1 85756 398 0

Phototypeset in 11 on 13 Sabon
by Keyboard Services, Luton, Beds

Cover design John Anastasio, Creative Line

Printed and bound in Great Britain by
Antony Rowe Ltd, Chippenham, Wiltshire

Jill Brook is partly the author, whose childhood may have led her – much later – to write 'Romantic' novels..

J M B

'... Nothing is worth more than this day ...'

Johann Wolfgang von Goethe,
Maxims and Reflections

CONTENTS

Poems

Poets and Children

No longer walking by streams,
Nor feeling the dew on our feet,
We roll names on our tongues,
Transfer them emblazoned in poems.
We write of 'dew and glory'
But our rainbows are gone.

Out of the bright-fringed noon sky
The Almighty speaks:
'Throw your runes in the river –
Go back to your woods!'

Seeking Enchanter's Nightshade,
Or a tiny arc of rainbow,
We go back.
Back over the fields
To our old woods –
Where new children roam
By stony brooks, at the foot
Of bracken-clad cloughs.

Their stepping stones lead to Paradise,
Where rainbows are magically brighter,
Nightshade more enchanting,
Than poets can ever make with words.

PRELUDE

Jill Brook is born 'a fortnight late' at tea-time on a December Tuesday, and must therefore have been conceived towards the end of the previous February.

As a result of the negligence of the monthly nurse who dashes off to another case – says her mother Mrs Brook – Jill begins to lose weight. Mrs B does not have enough milk and by the time Jill is weighed three weeks later she is two pounds less than her birth weight and vomits the cows' milk they decide to give her. She is taken to the General Infirmary, fortunately attached to a teaching hospital in the city, where for six weeks she is fed on solids. The specialist paediatrician saves her life.

Years later Jill discovers that a few years after saving her life he took his own.

Jill's mother visits her baby every day and by the time Jill is three months old she has turned the corner towards life.

There is a photograph of her in a cot in the hospital, and later snaps of a healthy-looking baby in the arms of various members of the family.

Jill's grandmother and her Aunt May, newly converted to Christian Science, have been praying for her. Her mother says later – 'You were a fighter.' Jill wishes she had not been forced to be one. Later, people call people like Jill 'survivors'.

The whole episode must have been a terrible blow to Mrs Brook's self-esteem, though nobody would have guessed. Jill becomes a plump toddler before becoming a thin little girl. Never again will her mother attempt to breast feed. Jill's new sister Nancy, born two years later – 'in a snowstorm' – is immediately given a bottle, and thrives. Neither does Nancy have Jill's later intermittent fear of hospitals, doctors, heights, and water, as well as other completely imaginary fears. But, as Mrs Brook often says, she takes after her paternal grandmother and Aunt May, the Christian Scientists. *They* are 'fuss-pots', not even brave enough to ride bicycles. Jill manages to ride a fairy cycle after many months of fallings off but she never learns to swim. Mrs Brook is a very good swimmer; she has no physical fears. Poor Jill's muscles all tense up in the effort to let go in the water. She has no confidence that water will hold her up. If human beings were intended to swim, why should it be so hard for her to float, and why indeed must she 'learn' how to float or swim? Before she is three years old Mrs Brook has taken her to ride on her back in the municipal swimming bath but Jill does not enjoy the experience.

ONE

The Dead Penny

When Jill is four, the old King and Queen ride through the town in an open car. Flags and bunting hang from the windows of Jill's house. That summer too there is a carnival in the park. Girls in lovely orange dresses, like silky crumpled poppies, dance on a raised stage, and one of them is singing 'Lily of Laguna'. Some of the girls wear hats like frilly lampshades. The dresses are what Jill will remember best. She adds the colour and the song to her favourite things – the tiny fizzy sweets called Swizzles, the large varnished sweets of 'rock', shaped and tasting like fruit – and buttercups.

There is a buttercup field in front of their terrace of houses, just across the road that passes the front gate of the garden. The field melts away into the town cemetery, separated only by a low dry-stone wall. Jill knows the cemetery well. It is one of her favourite walks, but somehow she never connects it with the end of the field, as they always walk to it by a continuation of the road and she never really looks over to it from the field.

The buttercups are on long slender stems and have brassy gold petals as well varnished as the sweet rock. Jill runs through the sea of flowers in a cotton dress that is printed with daisies and cowslips and for which she has knickers to match. Flowers are beautiful. She often dances around the garden chanting 'Mary, Mary.'

The cemetery is a pleasant place. Jill imagines the dead lying asleep with headstones for pillows, guarded by stone angels who will wake them at the last trump and take them over to the other side. One particular angel stands on a raised mound. She – for Jill always assumes angels are female – is of dazzling white, her robes trailing in clouds of marble, arms outstretched, marble veils floating from her wrists. Jill calls her Auntie May in her nightie, and indeed for some years confuses her with that aunt, her godmother.

On the cemetery walk they take the central path through the gates and turn left by the caretaker's lodge to the outhouse where there is water for their vases. Every Thursday the urns and glass vases are cleaned. They stand in a stone sink in the half dark, a greenish dark, pleasant after the sun's glare. Jill loves the stench of rotting flowers. It is not like any other smell she knows. She does not connect the smell with the flowers but with the place itself.

In the centre of the cemetery is a building bisected by an open arch. On the left as they walk through is the Anglican chapel and on the right the Non-Conformist one. No colour in those windows and Jill is sorry. The whole building is topped over the arch by a small belfry. Both Great-Grandfather and Great-Grandmother lie buried in the cemetery, primly on the 'Non-Con' side. Once or twice they vary the walk, after putting the flowers over Great Grandma S—, buried that very summer forty-three years after her husband (Nan says) and they walk further and further out, nearly to the wall. This is where Jill's buttercup field begins on the other side. She never looks over at her house from there. The boundary is in her mind; the cemetery is approachable only through its gates at the other end. When she is in the graveyard she does not even remember the buttercups or think that they have anything in common with the cemetery flowers.

Jill plays long hours in the buttercup field. Sometimes she is allowed to enter a long, low, wooden hut in the field near the road owned by Mr Taylor, a neighbour. This hut looks quite ordinary on the outside. Once inside though, and when you are accustomed to the dimmer light, it turns out to be a small aviary. The passion for budgies shipped over from Australia is at its height, and tiny green and blue bodies flit in their cages. Jill cannot decide which she likes best, the blue ones or the green ones. It is as difficult as choosing between buttercups and daisies, but in the end she decides for green. The tropical emerald and yellow are a delight to her four-year-old eyes, colours she will try to reproduce in her paint box. The blue is somehow safer, prettier – but not Jill's colour. Colours matter very much. The yellow and white of her dress delights her when she puts it on in the morning. She thinks the flower pattern almost unbearably beautiful... So many flowers, so many birds and of such dazzling colours!

She has a friend with the same name as her teddy bear, Edward, who lives nearby, and she sometimes plays with him in the field, though he is more often a winter companion for marbles. They play at the back of the houses in the lane and Jill is proud that he is her friend because he is eight. She does not like the other boys so much though she curries favour with them.

One summer evening they are out in the field. Edward is not there. Mr Taylor is around, going in and out of his hut behind which he grows dahlias and marguerites in the late summer. Michael and Peter and David are flipping pennies up and down, heavy pennies with George V regal on one side.

Suddenly one of them says: 'Show you a trick? I can throw that penny right away into the field and can make it come back again.'

'Go on – you can't!'

'Yes I can.'

'No, you can't,' Jill says, emboldened by the challenge.

'Want me to show you then?'

He flips the penny up in the air, catches it, and then throws it mightily. Jill follows its arc, as she thinks, wide over the field, over and over towards the cemetery itself, lost. Her eyes return to him, sorry that he has lost it. 'Come back, penny!' he shouts. He turns his palm over and shouts triumphantly: 'There you are! It's come back!'

Jill stares at his palm on which the errant penny has come to rest. She does not believe it. It could not have returned but it *was* there. How?

'How?' she cries.

'Ah! Wouldn't you like to know! It's magic, you see.'

'Do it again! Oh, do it again!'

He does it again. Again her eyes follow the penny over the field against the fading sky. 'Come home! Come home!' he calls. And the penny flips into place again on his palm. Jill is baffled and admiring.

Mr Taylor comes up. 'Oh, you know that trick do you?' he says.

'It's not a trick,' Jill says. 'It's magic... He made it come back!'

It was like one of those stories they told you at the Sunday School.

Mr Taylor laughs.

'Go on, you try it, Jill,' says John.

'Now, now,' says Mr Taylor.

'All right,' says Jill.

She has no idea what to do but she will show them she can. She expects it is something to do with believing. She will throw her penny (carefully saved to buy Swizzles at the little sweet-shop) and hers will come back if she wills it to.

Michael had shouted, 'Come back. Come back, penny!' That must have been the magic. Jill decides to do the same but to add a short secret prayer. She takes her penny out from under her sock, looks at it lovingly.

'No!' says Mr Taylor. 'Don't do it, Jill! You'll lose your penny.'

This makes her the more determined.

'Watch then,' says Jill.

She takes a deep breath, says to herself, 'Please God, send my penny back. Amen' – and then throws it with all her might over the long waving grasses, over to the cemetery, and shouts then:

'Come back! Come back, penny!'

She stands with palms outstretched, eyes shut, supplicating. Nothing happens. There is no welcome pressure in her palm. She opens her eyes. The others stare at her. She looks down at her palm. Empty. She waits, tries again: 'Come back. Come back ... come back ... penny.' She repeats the words desperately but knowing now that it never will.

'You don't know the trick,' says Mr Taylor kindly.

'It's magic,' says David.

'If it's magic it'll work for *me* then,' says Jill.

'Ha ha,' says John.

No, she knows it will not. It has probably gone over the far wall. Still, she can try to find it.

Michael giggles and points his finger at Jill. 'Lost yer old penny now,' he says. 'What'll your mother say?'

Jill won't be telling her mother, that's for sure. Throwing good pennies into fields is not Mrs Brook's idea of fun.

Her mother teaches her to write and do sums. Years and years ago Jill learned to read and now she does sums with tens and units, using little ladders, and counters you push up and over the ladders to make hundreds. With money you count in twelves not tens. This is only one penny, not sixpence or even a three-penny bit, but it belongs to *her*.

The boys drift off. She thinks they feel a bit sorry for her – but amused as well.

She runs into the grasses, beating them down and peering right and left. It is hopeless, but she won't give up.

The sun is even lower in the sky and the air darkening. She feels a bit like crying but doesn't in case the boys return.

It is not fair, she knows. They have deceived her, but she was a willing partner in the deception. Magic does not work for Jill. Her thoughts are muddled. Why doesn't it work for *her*? Because she is a girl? She will not try to be like them ever again.

She runs down further away into the grasses, not really looking any more. The precious penny has gone . . . The grass grows taller and pricks her legs spikily. She looks back and sees the buttercups. Then she looks ahead and sees the dry-stone wall. Perhaps she has thrown her penny so far that it is *over* the wall?

She runs towards the wall, puffing – and now she imagines the lone coin, greenish and dull and cold – but precious and hers.

Now she is at the wall, at the extreme edge of the field and for the first time in her life she begins to climb it. She bangs her knee, but she gets to the top and looks over. She sees the graves and the flowers all quiet and deserted. It is the cemetery. A curious shock pierces her dully. It has been there all the time. She forgets the penny. Nobody is walking up and down on the paths between the graves bearing flowers or carrying trowels. It is so quiet and odd. She is not lonely but she feels the graves are. What if she had died and lay under the ground in one of the graves? They look different in the evening.

She does not want to jump off the wall on the other side. They are in another place, the graves, and one she does not want to wander in alone. But she likes to look at them.

The sun is lower in the sky but it is still warm. She hears a car droning on the road and after a time she turns round slowly, carefully, jumps off the wall and lands back in a patch of daisies as the sun goes down in a little breeze and over the wall the dead sleep. They are so near, she thinks.

Her mother calls: 'J – ill!' and so she makes her way home.

She does look again for the penny another day and in her prayers has inserted a special request along with 'Pity mice implicity.'

'Please God, let me find my penny and don't let me die,

Amen.' She thinks that perhaps the penny too is in the cemetery.

Edward says, when she tells him about it: 'It's a trick. They never throw it. They keep it down their shirt-cuffs. You haven't got a shirt, Jill.'

As she thought – not a trick for girls.

TWO

Red Roses

'I have five big dolls, and a family of tiny dolls who live in the dolls' house. Santa Claus brought me a teddy bear two years ago. I have a lovely dolls' pram and a cot, and also a bicycle. Upstairs we keep a swing. I have clay, beads, a shop, a circus, a farmyard, pencil-sets, crayons, paints and a sewing box.'

That's what Jill writes when she is five years old in a black hard-covered exercise book. Mother is giving her lessons so that she need not go to school until the summer.

She also writes: 'Mummy loves us all tremendously.'

The child Jill holds tightly to the hand of an 'Auntie', but not the tall fair one whose husband, Uncle Sidney, is interested in plays.

Uncle Sidney likes Jill to dress up and do Cinderella at the Ball in the white muslin Princess Dress with the yellow sash and the gold cloak. Sometimes he pretends to be the Prince, and she likes to preen herself under his regard. He makes long speeches until Auntie Olwen says it is time to go home, and Mother says she mustn't get too excited.

But she can't help being excited this afternoon for she has been invited to a special theatrical garden-party. Uncle Sidney is somehow responsible for all this and there is mysterious talk of a Green Room which Jill imagines to be like the Sunday School Hall but all painted in bright emerald green, still her favourite colour.

It is a hot day and she is so excited that she cannot wait to do the job they have asked her for. Auntie Win holds a big basket in which are hundreds of red roses with silver paper stems. Jill has to take a rose and walk in front of the basket and stop people and say:

'Will you buy a rose for the Green Room Fund? They cost a shilling but you can have a bud for sixpence.' People smile and most of them buy a rose and put a shilling or sometimes a sixpence in the tin which is round Jill's neck and clanks as she walks. Her hand is too small to hold it.

Uncle Sidney has disappeared and she is getting tired and the auntie with the basket of roses says: 'Let's sit down. It's a fair scorcher.'

So they sit on an iron bench near a little lake and behind them there is a sloping place of grass which comes down from a little stage where some bigger children are going to play the 'Princess and the Woodcutter' after tea.

Jill has wanted to wear the Cinderella dress but Mother has said it isn't suitable and that's that. So she is wearing a flowery dress with big puffed sleeves banded in white and her best socks and sandals. Thank goodness not her winter velvet party frock which always gets things spilt on it, which makes her mother rage because marks cannot be washed out of silk velvet.

Jill looks at the roses lying now rather forlornly in the flower-girl's basket. She puts out a finger and strokes a dark red petal and it feels like stroking her winter party frock. She bends her head and sniffs and the most wonderful velvety scent envelops her, so strong and beautiful she feels there are no words to describe it.

'I wish I could have a rose, Auntie,' she says. 'But I haven't got sixpence, not even for a little one.'

'Wait till the end – they might give you one for helping,' murmurs the auntie, head back, eyes half-closed.

Just then someone says: 'Shoo!' and Jill turns round. A tall fair man is leaning over Auntie, tickling her nose with a long, dried grass stalk.

'Oh, *Everard*!' says Auntie Win and opens her eyes. He comes round and sits between the two of them.

Jill feels that he is rather rude as he never said 'Hello' to her and after all she is the flower girl. She rattles her collection-box and takes a big, beautiful blossom from the basket. She gets down from the seat and taps at the gentleman's knee.

He turns in a rather annoyed way. He is a very funny-looking young man but Jill feels sure he will give her a shilling. But he has turned back to Auntie Win.

'Please, Mister,' says Jill. 'Will you buy one of my lovely red roses? A shilling for a big one and a sixpence for a bud and they've got silver paper on and don't scratch.'

He says nothing and Auntie Win says: 'Why not have a little walk, Jill? Not too far, mind – take two or three from the basket and just walk up to the stage – you'll find some people there to buy, I'm sure.' She yawns.

Jill selects three large roses and touches her cheek with the petals. They are so soft and so scented. To think you can have all that for a shilling! She sees another auntie in the distance and makes her way in that direction, determined to make a sale this time. The first person she stops is an old lady who smiles and pats her head, but then says she has no change. Then a big boy comes up and laughs at her: 'Who wants mouldy old roses?' he says. That doesn't worry her. Boys are not normally interested in flowers. In the distance, coming down the path from the theatre she sees a big man who might be the sort of man who likes flowers. She struggles up the slope as he looms ahead. She can't put her hands on the grass because of the tin and holding the roses in one hand.

'Mister, Mister!' she shouts and sees as she comes up to him a dark face with two very brown eyes and a moustache. Her heart turns over. He is just as she had imagined the Prince – not Uncle Sidney, but the real one. She stops in front of him and smiles. 'Will you buy one of my lovely red roses? One shilling.'

The man looks down as if hardly able to believe his eyes.

'What next?' he says in a stormy voice. 'No, I won't. I need my *tea* – and my garden is *full* of roses.'

She stands, stunned, the roses pointing down to the ground and great scalding tears come up and she wants to sob, sob in Auntie Win's lap. It is not that he does not want to buy a rose – but the way he said it – so cross and nasty – as though it were somehow her fault. She feels ashamed to have offered him one as he turns away, brushing her aside, then she feels angry that he has been rude, and the tears of anger and shame choke her.

Just then a lady comes running up to the big man and says in a silly voice: 'Darling, come for some tea, do. It's so *hot*.' He looks at her the way he looked at Jill so she is sorry for the lady though her voice is silly and what they call la-di-dah.

'Simon,' cries a man's voice and the man who would not buy a rose turns, smiling.

Jill sees his face change as he goes up to his friend. The lady gives a shrug and mutters: 'Sell him a bloody pansy.' Jill has no time to think this over, for down the steps from the grassy stage comes Uncle Sidney.

'Ah, my little flower-girl, my little Princess – will Cinderella give me a rose?' He sweeps her up to his freckled face.

'It's a shilling,' says Jill. 'But the best ones are in Auntie Win's basket.' He puts her down, searches in his pocket for change and plops a bright coin into the box round her neck.

'Now come for some tea,' he says and she puts her hand in his. She sees Mother signalling in the distance. 'Jill will stay with me for tea,' shouts Uncle Sidney.

'You'd like some tea and to watch the play?' he asks.

'Oh, yes, but Auntie Win's basket?'

'*She'll* look after that.'

'Uncle Sidney – that big man down there – he wouldn't buy a rose. I thought he would. He'd look nice with a rose on his jacket, wouldn't he?'

Uncle Sidney opens his mouth and roars with laughter. 'Don't you worry, Cinderella,' he says, '*I'll* buy all your roses.'

'I thought that man was nice,' says Jill. 'But he *isn't*. I thought he would buy a rose.'

'He's an actor,' says Uncle Sidney shortly.

'But *you* are an actor, Uncle Sidney.'

'I'm no Prince Charming,' says Uncle Sidney.

Jill is not sure what he means. Certainly, he likes to play Prince Charming when she plays Cinderella, but he does not look like Prince Charming, though he is nice. That nasty man who didn't want the roses, now he *did* look like Prince Charming!

The five-year-old girl, Jill, looks up at her 'uncle'. 'You can have the rest of the roses for nothing,' she says. 'Auntie Win won't notice.'

But she is to remember 'Simon' often with a mixture of anger, embarrassment, longing and shame.

THREE

Uncle Bill and the Pink Blancmange

Very unlike 'Simon' was Uncle Bill Murgatroyd, a big, red-faced man with a wife called Auntie Una, a name Jill thinks odd. They have no children of their own but Mother says they 'love children'.

'Now, mind you behave nicely,' says Mother one day. 'Your Uncle Bill Murgatroyd and Auntie Una are coming to tea.'

As usually happens when they have visitors, the preparations are endless. You'd have thought the King was coming to tea. There is the slicing of the York ham – accomplished in good time before the guests' arrival, as her father is the sort of man who will cut his finger if asked to do any carving. Then there is the ceremony of making fruit jellies – not the sort you can buy in a packet, but ones made from gelatine and real fruit juice, with a raspberry or two idly floating in the bowl till it sets hard.

Mother always bakes on Thursdays and so there will be plenty of scones, oatcakes and sponge cakes already waiting in their neat tins. On this particular Saturday morning, Mother has decided to make a pink blancmange for she doesn't trust the ice-cream man to arrive at the right time –

and anyway 'bought' things are not thought suitable to offer to guests. The blancmange is an added bonus – usually jellies are enough. Mother must like Uncle Bill. She always feeds him well. 'Your Auntie Una doesn't do much baking,' she says with a sniff. Indeed, Auntie Una is a colourless lady with pale thin hair and pince-nez and a very quiet voice which she seldom uses. Uncle Bill usually does the talking. Still, Jill likes Auntie Una. She will sometimes smile quietly at Nancy and her with a longing look which Jill interprets as longing for the children she has never had. She is sorry for Auntie Una.

But she does not like Uncle Bill. She doesn't know why she doesn't like him – it is to do with his large voice and his large, beefy hands and his blustering red cheeks. Somehow her father always seems smaller in his presence, saying very little. Still, as her mother says, they went through the Great War together and are therefore bosom friends.

Before Uncle Bill and Auntie Una arrive that Saturday afternoon, Jill and Nancy are sent out to play.

But – 'Mind you come in when you're called to brush your hair and wash your hands before your Uncle Bill's arrival.'

Jill wanders outside disconsolately. It is never much fun playing out when you know there is a time limit. She keeps thinking of that lovely wobbly pink blancmange sitting on its crystal dish in the cellar, waiting for tea. She is rather a greedy child, usually hungry. Her mother does not believe in children being given sweets to eat and Jill is often the secret recipient of toffees and butterscotch and Pontefract cakes from kindly neighbours who show their affection in pandering to her sweet tooth.

Her father has also gone out of the house and is busy staking up some dahlias in the back yard. Jill doesn't know what impels her to say what she does, but after watching him for a bit and seeing no kindly neighbours around to take pity on her, she goes up to where he is snipping garden twine and in a burst of confidence, wanting to talk to someone, she comes out with:

'I don't like Uncle Bill Murgatroyd!'

He straightens up and looks at her levelly. She feels ready for more confidences on a person-to-person basis.

'I don't like him,' she says again, waiting expectantly for his reply.

'Now why's that?' he asks, searching in his pocket for a Gold Flake cigarette.

'I don't know,' says Jill. She thinks of saying that he eats too much or his voice is too loud, but it isn't true. She just doesn't like him.

'He's always very kind to you,' says Dad shortly. It's true. Uncle Bill *has* been kind. In fact he has once given her and her sister a whole half crown each, a fortune. (Unfortunately, it has gone straight into the Yorkshire Penny Bank.)

'Yes, I know. It's a secret anyway.'

'You've got plenty of secrets,' says Dad.

Jill changes the subject. 'We're having blancmange *and* jelly,' she says.

Her father laughs. 'Always thinking of your tummy.'

He hangs around for a bit, then goes inside resignedly to make a fire in the sitting room. In spite of its only being October, it is cold, though the sun has tried to come out earlier. Jill goes round to the front of the house where Nancy is playing a solitary game of her own. She looks round for some of her friends, the big boys who play marbles, but there is no one in sight except her sister. Marbles are not allowed Nancy as she might stuff them in her mouth and swallow them, being only two and adventurous in her tastes.

Across the fields she sees a wisp of smoke from an early bonfire. The boys are probably down there with their fairy cycles. It is too far for Jill to go to be within earshot of her mother. She'd better not risk it as she has her best dress on – her new winter dress of rust wool and her best brown shoes. How long till tea?

She finds the doll's pram pushed in front of the holly bush. In it her sister has placed her best doll and Jill's teddy bear. That morning Jill has married them in a long ceremony. Edward Bear is at the bottom of the pram on his face. Sylvia, with her real hair and her eyes that close and open, is lying against the pillows rather stiffly. Jill picks up Edward and changes their places around. There is no room for them both against the pillow. On second thoughts she picks Edward up again and sits on the step to tell him a story about a tea-party with jelly and lemonade and cake and a giant blancmange.

She hears her parents talking in rather angry voices inside the house and then a door slams.

It is some time later when Jill is beginning to feel bored as well as hungry that she is called in.

'And for heaven's sake stop that fire from smoking!' shouts her mother. She is all flustered, with her apron still on, but her lovely black hair is shining and under her apron she has a nice yellow dress and her best silk stockings. Soon everything is ready and on the stroke of three as Nancy and Jill are just about to get up and look through the window, the door-bell rings. The fire is burning brightly, the table is set, Mother's apron is off and hanging in the kitchen, and Father gives a twitch to his tie, catches his reflection in the mirror and smoothes his hair. Mother opens the door and they crowd round behind her.

Uncle Bill and Auntie Una are, of course, always punctual. In fact Uncle Bill is just putting away his big gold watch in his waistcoat picket before he swoops down and snatches up Jill and then her sister and gobbles a kiss on their cheeks before putting them down to say 'Hello' to Auntie Una, who is waiting quietly behind him in a grey coat and hat and knobbly shoes.

'Come on in then, Bill, Una.' Jill's father bustles about taking coats before the two men go into the sitting room to sit by the now glowing fire.

'Tea'll be ready soon,' shouts Mother, piloting Auntie Una up to 'wash her hands'.

Jill and Nancy hang about, peep in the dining-room to look at the table, fetch their reading books to 'read to Uncle Bill'.

'I can act Cinderella,' says Jill to Uncle Bill.

'Not now, love,' says Father. 'Save it till after tea.'

Jill sits on the pouffe behind the sofa that her father calls a Humpty Dumpty. Nancy comes in on Auntie Una's hand, looking pleased with herself.

'Such lovely curls,' Auntie Una is saying. Uncle Bill takes it up as they come in.

'Nancy can act Goldilocks,' he says.

Nancy's hair is fair and curly whilst Jill's is mousy and straight, but Nancy can't act Cinderella. That is Jill's party piece. Jill goes to the lavatory while they go on about Nancy's hair.

It is not long before the whole company is led into tea. The blancmange is on a side table surrounded by small jellies. Father busies himself pronging ham and mother hands round the china teacups and the mugs for Nancy and Jill, hers blue, Nancy's pink. Jill looks fondly at her mother and father. Even Uncle Bill seems bathed in a mellow light from the kitchen range. Auntie Una is nibbling bread and butter in tiny mouthfuls, leaving no crumbs on her mouth.

Jill stints on bread, butter and ham to leave more room for the glory of blancmange and jelly. Uncle Bill has two helpings of ham and many cups of strong, sweet tea.

'Jill – you can help serve the next course,' says Mother, and Jill is over in a trice. Mother divides up the blancmange and Jill takes a plate to Auntie Una, who smiles vaguely. There will be plenty for them all. How Jill looks forward to that blancmange!

'Ho, ho,' says Uncle Bill. 'None for me then of your mother's lovely blancmange?'

Jill takes him a plate and he leans towards her. 'Sure you want me to have it?' he says. 'A little bird told me you don't like me.'

Jill is rooted, thunderstruck, the blow seems to leave her head and land in her stomach. There seems to be a sudden well of silence, Jill holding the plate over to Uncle Bill and her father leaning back and Auntie Una with her face cast down and Nancy still eating her bread.

Mother looks at Jill quickly and takes the plate from her,

depositing it firmly in front of Uncle Bill. She seems about to say something. Jill looks at Uncle Bill and at the blancmange and feels terrible tears coming up her throat to strangle her. He knows. How can he know? Only her father knows that she doesn't like Uncle Bill. Mother looks inquiring, then angry. Then they all laugh. Ho. Ho. Ho.

'Of *course* Jill likes you,' says Mum.

They are waiting for Jill to say something.

'Yes,' Jill says. 'I do like you – I like you very much.' She adds, 'May I get down, please?'

Uncle Bill laughs and says, 'Give me a kiss then.'

Grown-ups are very odd; they want to be liked, and she feels guilty that she does not really like him, without knowing the reason, and even more guilty that she has said so to Father. She has the queer conviction that Mother does not like Uncle Bill either. The heavens do not open to swallow her and her fib. The grown-ups resume their conversation and their eating. Auntie Una even pats Jill's arm.

As for Jill, mixed with the terrible fear that Uncle Bill can perhaps read her thoughts – though he is now smiling at her and chucking her under the chin – she is blushing, heart pounding, appetite gone, the pink blancmange untouched on her plate. How could she have hurt poor Uncle Bill's feelings, how could she make it up to him now? Surely it was better to fib and fib and fib than hurt a person's feelings? Who has told him? Anger fills her as well as shame – and shame at her own discomfiture.

After tea Uncle Bill draws Jill to him. 'Sit on your old uncle's knee, then?' he says.

Jill complies, but her head hangs and the tears are for him. Later that evening she is sick – so in a way she is glad she has not eaten her share of the blancmange. She has it on the Sunday.

There are many things you must not say, so that you do not hurt people. Often though, she is caught up in some embarrassment and suffers shame on others' behalf.

Some friends of her parents' have a relative who lives with them and who has a large, red, lolloping birthmark on one cheek. The first time the three-year-old Jill sees Joe he frightens her. Somehow she knows he is nice underneath so instead of screaming her head off she says politely to her mother,

'Can I go and play with Lizzie, please?' Mother is aware of the reason for the request and Jill is allowed to join the maid in the kitchen.

Later, she hears Mother say to Father, 'It was clever of the child – I know he frightened her, but she wouldn't say. I asked her on the way home and explained it was a birthmark and do you know what she said? – "I didn't want to hurt his feelings!"'

FOUR

Learie and the Marbles

Men fascinate Jill.

First of all her father, Daddy, in his big armchair with wooden arms on which he balances a packet of Gold Flake cigarettes. Sometimes he takes Jill to the public library with him but when he is in his armchair he never answers her questions from behind his book or newspaper but gives only a mumbled semi-groan until she stops trying to get him to reply.

There are other kinds of men, men who *do* things, like the lamp-lighter who comes round in winter before tea-time with his long pole that is a magic wand when it puts the lights on.

Jill waits for him to arrive in the early dusk. As far as she knows he does not come in summer, for then it is too light and she has had to go to bed while the sunlight is still in the world.

Because she has read and heard a poem about a lamp-lighter in a small green book called *A Child's Garden of Verses*, she calls her lamp-lighter Learie, like the man in the poem. She thinks of him as Learie Smith or Learie Robinson with Learie as his first name like Leslie or Roy. He is a kindly man, quite old, she thinks, with a red nose. Later, the scarecrow in *The Wizard of Oz* reminds her of Learie. He talks to her more than anyone and she will chatter endlessly to him because she thinks he has already realised that she knows him from the poem. Indeed one day she mentions the poem, but he does not understand what she is on about and just changes the subject, quite kindly.

When Learie comes upon her on winter afternoons she is often playing marbles with John and Edward. She is very proud of her marbles, in their special bag, particularly the 'taws' and the one sepia marble with white flecks. Each marble is something special and beautiful. Most of the best ones are of opaque glass like the sepia one, but in colours of pale jade, sky blue, 'Chinese' yellow, orange and white. The best is the red 'blood alley' which counts for more, and John has a 'Queen', Edward a 'King' which are the biggest marbles she has ever seen. The blue alley is made of *real* marble, not glass, and she has only ever seen one like that. Cheaper marbles are made of transparent glass. Even cheaper are the wooden marbles and the brown stony ones. The transparent ones have just one wiggly stripe of colour to make them pretty. The thick taws are more valuable because you can't buy them very easily; they are older and lie heavy in the marble bag. She is the only girl she knows who plays marbles. It is like conkers in October. The boys always have bigger, harder ones on better pieces of string, but Jill has asked her father to help her make some that year and she has beaten a few of the boys.

John and David are older than her and have fairy cycles while she only has a tricycle. She isn't frightened of these boys; they are nice to her and sometimes let her win a game. She will often go with them to the little shop up the road and into the lane behind the terrace. It is a sort of post office but has lots of delicious sweets in its windows. Jill loves sweets and always spends her Saturday penny on them, usually on Swizzles.

Once she steals a halfpenny from Mother's purse to buy them: the guilt is unbearable.

What worries her most, even though Mother never discovers the theft of the halfpenny, is that she will not be able to tell Father Christmas that she has been 'a good girl'. He always asks that. She is convinced that, like God, he knows everything, and asks her only out of politeness.

When the lamp-lighter comes he will watch her playing. She does not play a very complicated game but the boys don't seem to mind and she will kneel or squat in her brown ribbed stockings and flick her marbles in the dusty muddy back lane. But she does not win very often because the boys are older and although they would not play the trick of the returning penny upon her, they must get tired of such an easy opponent.

She sees John and David as grown men, infinitely superior to herself, so much older are they – eight or nine years old! Edward wants to be a bus conductor. John is unsure.

She must have once complained to the lamp-lighter that she could never win, for one day he takes pity on her and yet at the same time enjoins her not to use the weapon he is giving her. This is, she feels, curious.

What happens is this:

Learie comes round one Tuesday in November at about half past three when it is already getting dark. It has been a little misty all day and Jill has felt as dull as the day, heavy and leaden. She has also lost her best marble, the sepia special one with the white flecks. This makes her feel guilty as she always does when she loses anything, which is often. She never speaks of her losses to her mother or father, fearing she will be blamed, and blaming herself enough already.

She has been waiting in the front room, for Learie comes that way on his rounds. The main gas lamp is outside No. 17 on the other side of the road and Jill always stays at the window looking for the first sight of him before tea. In October he is after tea, but in November just before. She catches sight first of the pole over his shoulder, waggling high, and then of course Learie himself appears on his bicycle, riding stiff and straight. He dismounts and leans the bicycle against the wall of the long field and then he shifts the pole from his shoulder to his hand and swiftly touches its high end to the mantel at the top of the gas lamp. Once he did it sitting on his bicycle, according to her father, but Jill has not seen this. One of the other lamp-lighters carries a ladder with him for repairs, but Learie just comes on his bicycle with the long pole.

Jill often thinks of this pole as a magic wand, since it makes light in dark places. It is like a touch-paper, the blue paper that Father lights the fireworks with – a stubby red and grey glowing end. But the lamp flowers into something more than a silver fountain or golden rain. It becomes a crystal glitter and the different lamps strung along the road are like a necklace of jewels when you look out at them from the bedroom window once it has become really dark.

On that November Tuesday, Learie is a little late and when his pole is finally glimpsed it does not stop at the light but instead carries on walking, held in Learie's hand. She runs to the door and opens it and sees Learie's bicycle propped up against the dry-stone wall of the field opposite and then sees that Learie is also putting the precious pole down next to it. He rummages in his pockets.

'Learie,' she shouts. 'Why haven't you put the light on? Wait for me!'

Learie looks up and looks away as though he is a bit shy. 'Come here, I've got something for you,' he says at last.

'Oh, what is it? Show me!' Jill is over the road in a tick.

'Shut your eyes and put your hands out,' he says when she reaches him, out of breath. 'And mind, it's heavy!'

She holds out her hands and suddenly something heavy and round and cold, oh so heavy, is in her cupped hands.

'Can I open them now?'

'Aye.'

She looks down into her hands and sees an enormous crystal ball, bigger than the biggest marble, as big as a tennis ball, and solid.

'What is it, Learie?' she asks. 'Is it for me?' She says that in case he just wants her to admire it and is going to take it back with him.

'It's a present. You'd beat 'em *all* with that, all the boys – but it isn't for playing with – they'd say it wasn't fair. But it's for you. Do you like it?'

'Oh, Learie, it's lovely. But what is it?'

'It's an old gas bulb – see how heavy it is?'

'Does it light up?'

'Nay!'

'But it's so big. Can I really have it?'

'Aye – I've told you. It's a present.'

'But I shall have to give *you* a present. Would you like a sparkler?'

'Nay, keep your fireworks. That's just a little extra present – now I'm off – I'm late as it is!' He seems a bit cross and she doesn't know *what* to say, to convey her amazement at the glass ball – the Big Marble. So she carries it carefully across the road and dares not put it down as she watches Learie light the lamp.

'Thank you, thank you,' she shouts again. 'I'm taking it inside.'

'Be careful,' he shouts back. 'Don't you crash it now!'

Jill feels the responsibility of the Big Marble lying very heavily upon her. It is too big to go in the old marble bag and she dare not leave it anywhere in case it rolls away.

'You'd better put it in your toy drawer,' says Mother when consulted.

'But I want to show it to Edward!'

'Well, you show it to him tomorrow and then put it back, mind.'

Jill can hardly wait till the next day dawns so that she can go to the back yard and the lane with the boys. Unfortunately, it is raining and she has to wait a bit. Pressing her nose against the kitchen window she watches the rain churn the yellow mud in the yard. She holds the glass in both hands – oh, it is heavy! Then she holds it on the sill and sees that when the light comes on to it you can look through it and see rainbow colours. If only it were not so heavy she could hold it up against the light and see if it turned things into rainbow-bordered surprises like the carving knife and fork rests do when you squint through them.

When the sun finally comes out she emerges from the back door carrying the bulb like a new-laid egg.

'What's that?' asks Edward with no ceremony, whisking round on his one roller skate and almost knocking her down.

'Oh, be careful – it's my new marble – it's the biggest marble in the world. It'll beat every other marble. It was a present – from Learie.'

'Who's Learie?'

'The lamp-lighter man.'

'Oh, you mean Benny Hoskins. Any road *that's* not a marble. It'd be cheating to play with that.'

'Well, I *won't* play with it then. But *if* I did it'd beat everybody.'

Jill feels the curious injustice of having to deny herself the pleasure of beating everyone since the Big Glass is too big, unfair; it doesn't count.

The boys are at first respectfully interested, then say they've seen things like that before, say finally that they'd swap it for a broken roller skate, six ordinary marbles and an apple. Jill holds on to it, glorying in its uniqueness, determined not to part with it, but cross at its uselessness. The others start a marble game so she takes her present home and wraps it in a handkerchief, fetches her ordinary marble bag and loses repeatedly to John. When she loses she threatens to bring out the Big Crystal Ball but the chorus of 'It wouldn't be fair', prevents her.

She often thanks Learie for it and lets him know it is close to her heart, but many years later she swaps it for a leaky black fountain pen.

FIVE

Jill and her Parents, the First House and the First School

Jill often sits on the 'buffet', the Humpty-Dumpty-like stool, and looks at her knees. The inside and outside creases are different. She also examines her hands, and wonders, who am I?

It is peaceful just to sit and think in the front room of the First House before guests arrive. If it is winter there is a fire and she stares into it, the warmth of the fire the next best thing to sun. There is an oval mirror hanging in the room but it is too high for her to see herself in it. Once or twice she sees herself in the hexagonal mirror in the bathroom and it is an odd feeling: this is me, behind my eyes is me, but where am I really?

When relatives or guests come to tea, she shows them her cigarette card albums and her whip and top – she has chalked the top herself – and the book she is reading. Some of the cigarette cards are of people with funny names who sing or make jokes on the wireless. Her favourite is a lady with golden hair called Wyn Ajello.

Jill knows that her mother is 'clever'. She is not the sort of person who will heap praise on her children though. You do what she asks because she can be frightening when she is angry. But she is pretty, and can make grown-up people laugh. She married Father because he 'fell in love' with her. Mother's thick dark hair is parted in the middle and she has deep-set eyes, a straight nose and a mouth that she puts lipstick on when visitors come. Unlike Auntie May she does not like jewellery, and doesn't use scent except for, now and then, a dab of 4711 Cologne from the bottle with a greeny gold label on her dressing-table.

Mother is a good singer and dancer and very brave, and she is also a good needlewoman and knitter. Indeed she is what *she* calls a 'good all-rounder.' Everyone says what a good teacher of little children she was before she married Father.

'Your mother could have been an actress,' one uncle says to Jill. One of Jill's early ambitions is therefore to be an actress. Jill says to Uncle Sidney, that his wife, Auntie Olwen, can be one of the Ugly Sisters when they next act Cinderella. When people laugh, she realises what she has said. It is her second social embarrassment after the one with Uncle Bill, and she wakes up in the night wondering why she said it. It is not that Auntie Olwen is ugly; she was trying to be polite, giving her a part to play – and everyone knows that only *young* girls are Cinderellas. Of course the prince is young too – and nice Uncle Sidney is not.

If Mother enjoys talking to visitors, Father is much quieter. Guests listen to Mother and laugh a lot at what she says. There is no doubt about it, Mother is cleverer and prettier and quicker than Auntie May, and makes people laugh more, even if she also makes her and Nancy cry as well.

Father is a 'reader,' a good gardener and a composer of both verse and music for songs. He also enjoys painting in water colours. He says his time in the Flanders trenches has 'marked' him for ever, says he did not understand until then what 'most men were like'. So long as he can come home from his work at the family mill, have his high tea – and then stretch out in his big wooden-armed chair, hide behind the *Times Literary Supplement* and smoke a packet of Gold

Flake, he is happy. He is a contented kind of person. He is also concerned with outdoor things, likes going for walks in the woods and making visits to Woolsford on bustling Saturday afternoons. At school, a man – the headmaster – will be the one who punishes and canes and shouts, but Father is not that sort of man. Father is not impatient; Jill has inherited that defect from her mother. Mother is impatient to get things done. She is the one 'in charge', and Father leaves most things to her, except gardening and putting coal on the fire and polishing the family shoes.

Jill loves her father, but he is not involved in her life the way Mother is. Mother is concerned with things like cleaning and shopping and cooking and sewing and knitting and darning and telling you what you ought to do.

She knows her mother and father are very different, not just because one is a man and the other a lady, one with light brown hair – though there is not much of it left – the other dark.

Jill is an early reader, taught by her mother in the intervals between dusting, cleaning, washing and baking. Everyone says Jill looks like her mother, and she also talks a lot, like her. But 'inside', in spite of being a 'chatterbox', Jill is sure she is more like her father. Nancy, two years younger, is less clumsy, less talkative, what they call 'deep'. You never know what she is thinking. She is less like either parent – more patient than Mother and Jill, less liable to 'enthusiasms' than Jill and Father, who are sentimental and 'romantic'. Mother and Nancy are more practical.

'You take after your Auntie May,' says Mother, because Jill is not brave. But Jill knows she is bold in other ways, which May is not. Like Auntie May, however, Jill loves jewels and scent and flowers and cats and walks in the country.

'I like a child with spirit,' Mother often says, after she has smacked her for disobedience. When Jill sobs from rage after arguments with Mother, it is often gentle Aunt May who soothes her, who will always listen to what she has to say and let her sit on her lap.

Later, at school, other children talk about their 'Mams' who seem to be often furious or cross, so Jill knows that anger must be part of being a mother. She loves her own mother but has learned to hide many things from her, fearing disapproval or punishment. Some of these things she tells Auntie May, and some her father, and some no one. She knows she is two-faced; nobody knows all her real feelings, not even Auntie May who is too good to understand a bad girl. Her mother might understand them but Jill does not want to let down her guard. She knows she has a certain capacity for tale bearing, for she both hates and loves authority, keeps in with it when necessary, but is angry when it seems as if it might take away her own freedom.

'I'm like Mummy,' she says to her aunt, when Auntie May is being sympathetic. Mother calls this sympathy 'spoiling', and often says that Grandpa Brook 'spoils' Granny too. Mother often criticises Father's family and never stops saying they 'spoil' Jill and Nancy. Jill and Nancy however continue to feel loved by their Brook grandparents and Aunt May. Granny and Grandpa Brook are very kind people and Jill loves being with them. Her other grandparents, her mother's parents, are quite nice, but Grandpa Wood rarely says much. He is a short, robust, athletic old man and his wife, Nanny Wood, tells Jill that her mother was always 'the apple of his eye'. Perhaps he 'spoilt' her?

Jill will try both her parents on for size to see where they fit, will imitate them both.

Mother does not go in for enthusiasms, but it was when she was singing that Edwin fell in love with her, she says. Ever since, she has tried to sort him out, suggest he retrain, become a librarian, 'stand up to' his relatives... Mother tells them she once pushed their father into the swimming baths when they were engaged in order to show him she could life-save him.

Jill enjoys reading aloud, and that pleases the mother-who-once-wanted-to-be-an-actress, who used to give private elocution lessons to make a bit of extra money. Mother is good with money. Mother says Father does not care about money; he is not a spendthrift, enjoys it when it arrives but lets it go.

As well as being clumsy and badly co-ordinated, Jill is still losing possessions as well as her temper. She knows that she can be bossy too – like Mother – preferring sometimes to take the lead.

If Mother was once a teacher, and will be one again in the war, Father will always be a writer. By the time she is ten Jill will have been by turns an 'actress', a 'teacher', and a 'writer'.

The writing is to last the longest.

In the First House, a stone terrace house that they will leave when Jill is almost six and Nancy nearly four, they all eat their meals in the living room cum kitchen. A flight of stone stairs goes down from the adjoining scullery to a cellar where things are kept cool and where the coal also arrives down a hole they open in the yard. There is another ground-floor room on the other side of the house that looks out on a garden, but it is usually reserved for visitors or Sundays. In that room there is a settee, a footstool, the 'buffet', and two fat, round-backed easy chairs, upholstered in dark mauve velvet. Jill shivers if she runs her hand down the velvet.

Jill's mother, with the help of a cleaning lady who 'does the rough', spends a good deal of time and effort keeping these rooms clean, and the three bedrooms and the bathroom upstairs too. Dust from her exertions appears in large bands of speckled sunlight. Jill learns the words 'mote' and 'sunbeam' from her Father, but prefers her own word for it, 'fairy dust', since 'Sunbeams' are the names of the little girls who dance in pantomimes at Christmas. Jill loves the sun, and basks in it, standing at the window of her parents' bedroom, the room where she was born. The fairy dust falls on a thick book of her father's that lies on the chair beside his bed. The *Flax of Dream* it says on the spine of the book. That sounds magical.

One day from that First House Jill goes out for a walk with Mavis Taylor and her young man, past the windowless house with its peculiar long chimney, the house that frightens her; down Cow Lane over the fields to the brook, near the farm where bluebells grow. It is a pity you have to pass the frightening house to get to the bluebells, but once you are there, and Mavis and her friend Jim have swung you up and down between them, and you have hesitatingly but finally crossed the stepping stones, you are in a magic world. Jill has never seen so many flowers all at once and decides that blue is now her favourite colour. It is almost the same colour as the picture of Boy Blue above the words of her favourite nursery rhyme at the bottom of Aunt May's porridge bowl. He is asleep in summer fields like the hayfields near Speights' Farm, a picture you see only if you finish your porridge.

After they have picked some bluebells they walk over to see the new milking sheds which Mavis's boyfriend says are 'electric'. Cows are standing side by side with glass tubes that draw out the milk from their udders. Occasionally a soft moo escapes from the animals. Above the sheds is a notice which she spells out: 'T.T. Tested'. The cows smell of manure, she thinks, and the inside floor is muddy. But Jim says the notice means that the milk is clean.

'Can we go back the other way?' asks Jill, bored with milking machines and hoping to avoid the house on the way back.

'We could go up Meadow Lane and the long way round by the Estate,' says Mavis, who perhaps understands her fears. The Estate is a row of houses with small windows where the poor people live, and there are dirty children playing out in the road in front of the houses. Jill's short legs are tired, but she does not complain – anything to avoid the menacing silhouette of that chimney. But when they arrive back on the lane that leads home there is a smell of tar, and they see a steamroller going slowly up and down their road. The shape of the flat top of the steamroller with a chimney sticking up is not pleasant. Not as bad as the house, but still a little frightening. But Jill says nothing and escapes indoors to her mother who is giving Nancy her tea. Nancy is old enough now not to be in a high chair and she is always pleased to see her sister.

'Bread and Marmite,' says Mother.

Jill likes tea and breakfast best; it is dinner with tapioca or sago pudding that makes her feel sick.

Nancy spends a lot of time with a pair of blunt scissors making little mats by folding newspaper over and cutting holes in them. Jill is not patient enough for this sort of thing but is proud of Nancy's accomplishment.

'She'll be an artist,' Father often says of Nancy. Jill is marked out to be 'clever'. But now that Nancy is talking quite well they do things together with their dolls and their teddy bears and prams and dressing-up clothes.

When Jill is five and a half she goes to her first school. Mother has promised she will hear more tunes and poems there. By rights Jill should have gone to school six months earlier but as Mother was once a teacher she is excused for a time. There are two stops on the bus to go to school, and Mother and Nancy have to go with her four times a day, before Mother discovers another little girl who lives quite near who will walk with her. At dinner-time the teacher agrees to put her on the bus; the conductor will see she gets off at the right stop. For school, Mother buys her a brown velour hat and long beige stockings which are kept up by elastic garters at the top. Jill practises wearing them but they always fall down her thin legs and eventually her mother relents and sends her to St Cedd's in knee socks. But the brown hat has to be worn, though no other child wears a hat.

The teacher is called Miss Jackson and she does not teach the youngest babies' class but the next one up where you sit in rows on benches with low tables in front of you. The girls are bigger than Jill but they cannot read. Miss Jackson knows she can read, for Mother has told her. She is tall, with brown hair and a long nose, and quite kind. The teacher of the babies' class, which is also down some steps in the yard, is younger and prettier, with dark skin and black curly hair and a snub nose.

As her mother promised, they do a good deal of singing at school, where Miss Jackson plays the piano. Jill looks forward to 'When the harvest moon is shining'. All the best songs are about moon and stars and sun – yellow and orange and gold and silver songs. For a time, orange and yellow almost replace blue as her favourite colour.

Playtime is not so much fun; rough boys bang into you and there are lots of fights. The girls do not fight so much. Jill wishes she were big and strong and could hit some of the boys.

She does not stay very long at St Cedd's school for they are to move house soon and she is to go to another, bigger school.

SIX

Cinderella

Ever afterwards they say 'Do you remember when Jill was sick at the panto?' just as they used to say: 'Do you remember the time when Jill was sick in her winter coat?'

The winter coat was a thick teddy bear coat, warm and snug but somehow disgraced by her being sick in it. She has not been able to get home quickly enough from next door after the kind Taylors have taken her in their car to Doncaster and fed her with butterscotch. Mother has to put the coat in a bucket and Jill has cried and cried from shame. Being sick happens all over the place quite regularly so that Jill counts the parties and treats when she has *not* been sick as special triumphs. She has *not* been sick that time she is taken to see Father Christmas in the big Woolsford department store, but she has been terrified. She knows that Santa Claus will ask whether she 'has been a good girl' and she is ready with her answer 'Not always', but if he asks Mother, *she* will have to say 'No', and then Father Christmas will be so embarrassed and Jill won't be able to tell him what she wants for Christmas. It is with astonishment therefore that after she has passed through the grotto hand in hand with her mother and waited patiently in a long line for Santa, who is sitting on a big sack full of toys, Mother, on finally arriving before him, unhesitatingly tells the old gentleman – Yes, Jill has been good.

She is uncomfortably aware that a fib has been told – from her mother's point of view anyway, if not from her own. Father Christmas then dives into his sack and presents her with a doll's tea-set, so she has no time to formulate her list of requirements for Christmas morning, since, on hearing Mother's 'Yes', he says, 'You'll get what you want, my dear.'

How does he know? She would not mind being sick then as a protest.

It is especially sad that she should disgrace *Cinderella*. Jill has never been before to a real theatre and is too excited to take it all in. The excitement has been rising all day. Yesterday was an ordinary day except that Granny and Auntie May were round for tea. After she is tucked up in bed she has heard them talking for a long time and then Daddy has seen them off at the bus stop.

For weeks she has been begging, hinting and badgering Mother to take her to a pantomime. Kathleen next door has been to one before Christmas and now it is after Christmas and she still hasn't been, so in order to console herself she has pretended in a strange way to stop wanting to go and then become almost indifferent. She has wanted it so much that she cannot want it any more.

And now here they all are in a 'box' that Grandpa Brook has paid for and there is Grandpa sitting next to Granny who is eating an ice and looking out at the curtain from her round glasses, one of which has a dark glass because one eye is blind.

Jill sits in between Auntie May and Nancy. Mother is at the end of the box and Daddy is not there because he is browsing in the book shops. Grandpa has been able to get only six tickets. Nancy is really too young to be there but she is quiet and happy sucking her thumb. It is, Jill feels, the BIGGEST TREAT she has ever had, bigger even than the Yorkshire Dyers' party in Greetland which Kathleen next door's father took her to, along with Kathleen, of course. There was another Father Christmas there with a sack of toys and a bag of inexpressibly delicious pretend oranges and lemons made of a solid sugar that tastes like peardrops.

But this is It, this is The Theatre, and Jill keeps telling herself it is true; she is really here. All the way to the big town she has been too excited to speak and even now her stomach is all churned up with it.

'Oh, please God,' she prays, 'don't let me be sick!'

Until she was four she was so often sick, and even now she is just five she will sometimes feel suddenly horrible, not able to stop the sick coming.

The curtain rises but Jill does not at first recognise the story.

The Cinderella is in rags but then the Fairy Godmother arrives in pink and silver, holding a long long wand with a real star glittering at the end of it. More than anything in the world Jill wants a wand. She has pretended she has made one from an old pea-stick out of Father's garden shed but it does not really work. Real wands are magic. The Fairy Godmother is just now touching Cinderella – it has taken a long time getting to this, with Cinderella talking to Buttons and, before that, the Baron and the Ugly Sisters telling her off. The Ugly Sisters are really men in long skirts and everyone laughs a lot at them. Jill thinks they are not really very funny.

Oh, if only she could stop feeling sick. The fairy has made everything go dark and now there is the 'transformation scene' that Auntie May has pointed out on the programme. She swallows hard and concentrates on the idea of cold, icy cold, water which helps sometimes when she wakes up feeling sick in the middle of the night.

If the Fairy Queen was dressed in pink and silver with silver hair and silver wings, Cinderella is now standing on the stage in a pool of light and her hair is now long and golden and her dress gold and white, with puffed sleeves and a full skirt. Jill cannot see her slippers properly. And then on to the stage comes a coach with a little pony pulling it, and a coachman. Everyone claps and Cinderella gets into the coach and is pulled round the stage waving to the Fairy Godmother and then the curtain comes down, a real dark red plush curtain.

In the interval, Jill can hold it back no longer and is sick. Fortunately Auntie May has a paper bag with her and a big handkerchief.

'It was the porridge,' Jill moans. 'It was the porridge.' But she feels so much better after being sick that they let her stay. She feels so dreadful inside though – not in her stomach but in her mind – that she may have spoilt the outing for everyone. Auntie slips an arm round her and Jill sits through the second half of the pantomime, concentrating on the Prince – a lady with long legs and green velvet trousers. There is another lady dressed in blue and silver whom the Prince calls Dandini. Jill thinks Dandini is nicer looking than the Prince, and when at the end of the story Dandini arrives at the Baron's kitchen to try on the lost slipper, she almost expects Cinderella to marry him rather than the Prince.

After the curtain comes down for the last time Jill feels sick again and they rush her home in Grandpa's car, which does not help. She cannot believe it is all over.

She is like Cinderella – having to go home when things are not finished. When she goes to sleep, today will become 'yesterday' and she will be further off than ever from Cinderella. Even when Cinderella herself was on the stage, Jill has not felt quite 'there'. There seems to be more than one Cinderella. She has imagined it so often and played the part herself so often that it can't all be contained in this one pantomime, one stage, with one special girl being Cinderella. The book is better. It can happen again and again in a book – and the story is not spoilt by feeling sick.

She will always remember her first visit to the pantomime although she does not connect her real feelings with what everyone else seems to remember about it and wishes they would stop remembering her disgraceful sickness. Of course she has not forgotten that, but wants to hold on to the moment when the magic wand lit up the darkness and the moment when Dandini, all glittering in blue and silver appeared like another Fairy Godmother. The fear of rising sick goes on haunting her. Not when she is at home, though she is sometimes sick on quite ordinary days, but when she goes out 'for a treat'.

She makes a pact with God and Father Christmas – who resemble each other – that so long as she is not 'greedy' she will be spared feeling ill.

SEVEN

Fears

Feeling guilty is awful, and so is feeling embarrassed, but it is much worse to be frightened, though it does not last so long. Jill isn't brave, not a bit like her mother, the good swimmer who also enjoyed dancing and skating. Jill hates water and heights and slippery surfaces and never knows where to put her feet.

She is either excited or frightened, hardly ever in a neutral placid zone. Sweets and toys and the pantomime and her orange and yellow flowered dress have excited her, but there are seven things she has been frightened of before they leave the First House: the tall windowless house, the steamroller, the stagnant pond, the half-witted boy, the Bogey man, the dead cat and the dead leg.

The pond had green scum on it and never moved; it was in the hollow where there had once been a small quarry on the way to Nanny Wood's and she shut her eyes when they passed it. The funny boy with the big head who stared at you with his tongue lolling out lived near the pond. They said he was called Peter. Fright would mix with embarrassment in her if he ran to them, but Mother only said, 'Poor thing – he's an idiot,' and walked on, pushing Nancy in the pram. Sometimes he was in the farmyard near the post office and if she caught sight of him Jill would run in the opposite direction as fast as she could.

'He's harmless,' Mother said when she told her how he frightened her.

The pond and the boy were real things and so was the dead ginger cat in the gutter. She only saw the cat once but it was the shock of an animal lying there all stiff when she had not been expecting to see anything, that made her hair stand on end and shivers go down her spine, even before she realised what it was. She prayed to God that night to look after the poor cat in Heaven.

The Bogey man had lurked inside the folds of her father's dressing-gown hanging against the jimpey glass of the bathroom door. He probably lived in the loft where he made the skylight dirty. He might also be found behind the attic wall at Grandpa Brook's house, Holm Garth, where there is an inner door in the wall – and he looks out of the eyes of *The Laughing Cavalier*.

It was a thick wool dressing-gown with a tassel and she recognises it later when Father wears it on Sunday mornings, but when it was hanging behind the door she was sure it was a Bogey man.

That time it had been Father who had told her not to be silly, took her in the bathroom one morning and showed her the dressing-gown hanging quietly there. 'It looks different from the other side,' she said. 'At night.'

He laughed and said things could not change into people.

Every night she repeats aloud a long rigmarole to stave off danger. These are her 'prayers', or rather her monologue to the Almighty, when she offers him her promise not to cough, for a cough means Death. She hedges her bets by asking her teddy bear, Edward, to be constantly alert. Just as Grandpa and God and Santa Claus are connected, so are Edward Bear and a Guardian Angel. Edward guards her against bad men and nightmares.

'Please don't let me die in the night, don't count a little peff, it's not a proper cough.'

Jill tells her sister that two ladies live up in the loft above the stairs. It has a glass window laid flat on the ceiling.

'My lady is called Sarsama – what is yours called?' she asks that evening before they go upstairs to be in the room they share in the First House, which has two little beds with gold bedspreads.

'I don't know,' says Nancy, so Jill replies, 'Dih-Doh-Doh – that's what she's called,' and squeals with laughter. Later when she has tiptoed over the cold linoleum and jumped into bed with Edward Bear, Jill begins a long account of Sarsama's baking day. 'Yellow jam tarts and red jam tarts,' she intones. But Nancy falls asleep and adds nothing to the story that night.

Edward always sleeps with his head on her pillow. 'Keep watch. Good night,' she says every night, and kisses his brown nose. She loves Edward more than her dolls. He is in a way grown up, and responsible, and does not have to be looked after, unlike the dolls. Nancy's best doll is her own doll Barbara's sister, and is called Sylvia. The two doll sisters are often in hospital so that their owners can be nurses and bandage their legs and arms. All the dolls, and sometimes the teddies, the only boys in the company, go for walks in the garden in a small black pram.

It is there in that garden where her father teaches Jill something not to do with books and reading or adding up sums. He gives her a small watering-can so she can follow him round with his big one.

'No, Jill, not on their heads – the flowers drink up water from the ground – that's where their roots are.' She thought she had to pour water on to their open faces, though she could see no mouths, and is amazed. Then she feels embarrassed at her mistake, but Edwin laughs. 'They don't mind getting wet, but it's the earth that needs the water, not the flower tops,' he says. 'Look,' and he pulls up a flower and shows her its tiny thin root that had been right down in the ground. 'It isn't as pretty as the top,' she says, but tries to direct the water downwards.

Edwin and his sister May like gardening. Mother says she never has the time. It is Auntie May who explains to Jill that if you pinch off the dead rose another will grow later in its place.

'It's called dead-heading,' she explains. Jill thinks it sounds gruesome; she hates the word 'dead'.

Jill is always both excited and scared at the prospect of a party, just as she is afraid of dying in the night and of remembering the dead cat and the Dead Leg. A little later a new fear is connected with the Pig, who was a sudden heart-lurching shock.

There she had been in the farmyard on holiday at Hunsingore when somebody, probably one of the farm boys, said, 'Have you looked over the stable door? We've got some new piglets.'

Jill and Nancy had clamoured to see them and it was Father who held up Jill first to look over the three-quarter door that was too high up for her to see alone. And, just as she peered, in the split second while her eyes were taking in the dark, there was a sudden movement and a great snout and an enormous pink face was thrust at her, its jowls trembling and its little eyes staring hatred. It was huge, enormous, bigger than she had ever imagined an animal. She let out a scream and the pig lunged back. Of course Daddy put her down before you could say Jack Robinson but she went on screaming and sobbing from shock. She hadn't minded pigs before. But this sudden hurtful, *hating* animal thrusting his face into hers when she had only expressed polite interest; the way he had almost swallowed her up in his fury, blotted everything else out for that split second, and was to haunt her nightmares for years. It was so unfair – she had had nothing against the Pig and he did not like her. What had she done wrong for the Pig to lunge at her like that? And anyway it was their fault – they ought to have known that pigs were not safe, that they reared up suddenly, hated anyone looking into their sty.

But what she had really hated was the shock, the suddenness of it, the no-warningness of it – and she had been ashamed of her own sudden terror.

* * *

OLD TERROR

The sty door opened at the top.
He held me up to see the pig –
Who jumped – his face thrust hard and big
At mine. A flame licked down my spine
And pricked through every vein. I screamed.
'The pig was cross,' they said, 'a shame.'

One lesson then was learned at six
Though other terrors soon transfixed:
High slides, and water cold and deep –
One slip, I'd fall! I vowed to keep
My feet on land, nor climb, nor jump,
Shun dogs that barked, rough boys who thumped.

Then bit by bit these terrors fled,
Though buried deep. I thought them dead.
If sometimes they – in long nightmares
Of strangers' feet upon the stairs –
Returned, in general they were licked:
Ancient fears, childish panics.

Till burglars rapists muggers knives
Came back into new children's lives:
And death and violence stalked the land,
And old fears turned our hearts around.

* * *

The same suddenness had frightened her a year or two before

this. Approaching the bus stop at the corner with her mother, Jill had looked in the gutter – and seen a human stockinged leg. There it lay, a severed limb, suddenly presented as she looked down. She froze with anguish.

Mother said, 'What *is* it? What *is* it?'

Jill turned and buried her head in Mother's coat, unable to speak. Mother looked down in the gutter where Jill had been staring – how had she not seen it immediately? – and then laughed and said, 'It's only an old stocking!'

'No, no, it's a leg! A lady's lost a leg!'

'Jill, look, look! I promise it's nothing to frighten you.' But she would not look.

'Too much imagination,' said Mother, irritated.

Jill kept her head averted till the bus came and was slowly persuaded it *must* have been a stocking or else they would have taken it away. Several weeks later however, she was still having nightmares, seeing the thick leg, covered in the coarse brown stocking lying in wait for her when she looked downwards.

The Leg had happened before the Pig and they were both horrible because they were unexpected. People were sorry about the Pig who had only laughed at the Leg.

Everyone else seems to love the deep, green-tiled stone-bottomed swimming bath in the town. She thinks, it *should not be there*, in an ordinary looking building with a roof, looking like a house outside, but smelling sinister. She loathes its echo and chill and cannot imagine anything more horrible than having to undress, shivering, and come out of the little cubicle door and see it lying there in wait for her with its worshippers already in it, immersing themselves, shouting to the rafters. The chlorine makes her choke and the cold makes her gasp and only after the greatest persuasion is she ever willing to go down the steps at the shallow end, hold on to the side and let the water come over her waist.

For years and years it seems, through family expeditions and school parties and seaside holidays on the Yorkshire coast, she has to suffer it, her teeth clanking with cold and terror. She hates the water – it is just as terrifying being towed along on a rope and told to do leg-movements in the bracing waters of the North Sea, in a special pool for learners scooped out of the shore and filled with sea water – and it is freezing there too. Yet at least the sea has always been there. Nobody built it and you can just paddle and be left alone. To be expected to enjoy the swimming bath is inexplicable, but school swimming lessons are to be endured. Left in the shallow end as the years go by, Jill tries every week to summon up enough courage to get her feet off the bottom. They go on telling her that swimming is pleasurable. Even when after many summers she does get them off for a few moments, she holds her breath and flails along too quickly, arriving exhausted at the other side of the 'breadth'. She comes to the conclusion that cold water and herself do not mix, and tries not to mind that she is such a coward.

The look of things is very important. If things have a strange shape she feels they are menacing: that strange steam-roller for example, with its tall thin chimney; and that narrow house without windows they always passed on their way to the farm. She thinks of it as the Crooked House from a story she has read. It too has a long high chimney – and no face. Mother says it has windows on the other side but Jill dares not look for them.

The inexplicable dread she feels at passing the house is buried deep and only surfaces years later, when, the years having seemingly eroded the soil of the past, she will quail at the sight of an innocent-looking church on a low Oxford horizon. It was not a church but a water-tower or a sewage plant, some strange whim having enclosed it in nineteenth-century neo-Gothic. When you looked through one of the narrow windows, expecting to see an aisle and pews, you saw instead only a thirty foot high steel and iron skeleton, blocking in the whole building from floor to high roof.

The shock will remind her of long-ago fears. *It was not what it seemed.*

The event which ends her early childhood is connected

with a fear, almost the last of the fears she cannot express, though she admits it to herself. They have been living nearly two years at the New House and she is eight and a half when she and Nancy are asked to be bridesmaids. They are to carry Mavis's train down the chapel aisle in the full gaze of the public. Jill is sure she will do it wrong, but just as sure, right till the last moment, that she will never have to do it.

They have put on their bridesmaids' dresses of white net over taffeta with the rows of turquoise silk ruffles, and puffed sleeves; and put on their stiff white sandals over white art silk ankle socks. They have marvelled at the silver-paper-covered nosegays of pink rosebuds they are to carry, and at the rosebud and forget-me-not hair bands on their heads. In the taxi to the chapel, Jill has caught sight of a large field by Grassy Lane, full of buttercups, and suddenly been overwhelmed by their beauty. Even then, halfway to the chapel, she is saying to herself over and over again that, in the end, she won't have to do it. Something will happen to stop it. They won't be needed. They will be able to take off their lovely dresses and be forgotten.

So that when they actually arrive in the town and the taxi draws up and the crowd goes Ooh and Aah, she already feels it is happening to someone else.

Then there is a long blank. They must have waited for the bride and joined in to her procession, holding up her train, but Jill only 'comes to' in her mind when it is all over and still doesn't really seem to have happened. There is suddenly no more fear. It went when her feet carried her down the aisle behind the bride in spite of herself. She gave up her will and something else took over. For this she is grateful.

Now they can all relax and eat sherry trifle and be given little silver bracelets and be teased by the Best Man.

Other fears will go on but mostly now in nightmares. Jill often wakes up screaming from one, and it is always her father who comes in to soothe her. She clutches him like a drowning man on a raft.

'You ramble in your sleep,' her father tells her.

Jill's worst nightmare occurs the same year as she is a bridesmaid and it concerns Father. She dreams she is at home in bed when she is alerted by some noise, some disturbance. Then the front door bell rings, so she gets up, looks over the landing banisters and into the hall.

Her father is walking to the door, which he opens. Standing there is a man whom Jill knows to be a 'Bandit from Blackpool'. He is wearing a tall straw hat, and she sees that he is carrying a gun. Her father is about to let the man in – he has not seen the gun. She tries to scream, 'Daddy! Daddy! Look out!'

She cannot save him.

The bandit raises his gun and shoots her father, and she wakes screaming.

Over and over she says to herself:

'I couldn't save him. I couldn't save him.'

She tells him later what the nightmare was about.

EIGHT

Holm Garth, the White Swan, and the New School

While they were waiting for the New House to be built not far away, they were living for nine months at Holm Garth, Grandpa and Granny Brook's lovely big house. Jill was six years old by then and was shown the way to walk to the new school about a half mile away across the Stray. Auntie tells her it is named after the big Stray in Harrogate.

The first day at dinner-time, going home for dinner, Jill takes the wrong turning. She tries not to panic, retraces her steps to the school, somehow finds the right way and walks across the Stray.

On the way back to school, once you have crossed the Stray, there is a row of shops, the most enticing of which is the newsagent and sweet-shop. Here Jill discovers something better even than Swizzles. It is called Kali, a sort of sugary powder, not quite sherbet because it has crystals. You can have either Lemon Kali or Raspberry Kali or Rainbow Kali, a mixture of pink and yellow, and for a halfpenny you can buy a bag of it to stick your finger in and suck. Some people add it to water for lemonade, but Jill prefers it neat.

Mother takes her to the new school on the first morning, and explains to the new teacher that Jill can read proper books. But the teacher gives her a *picture* book to look at while she and Mother talk. Jill is disgusted. Perhaps the teacher doesn't believe Mother?

The classroom is up some stairs and Jill is given a desk at the back near the window. There are more children in the class than there were at St Cedd's and every morning they chant their tables in sing-song voices, girls holding hands across the aisles. The new teacher, Miss Blackthwaite, is quite tall, like Miss Jackson. She has a brown wavy bob, round-rimmed glasses, and sticking-out teeth. Jill finds her very sympathetic.

The children are divided into four groups, each with the name of a bird and a colour. Jill belongs to the Nightingales, who are yellow. The other birds are Swallow, Swift and Wagtail – red, blue and green. She likes the name Nightingale best.

Jill enjoys the new lessons: History, which begins with Eo, the boy who lived in a tree, and Geography where they draw circles for the earth and coloured bands across the circles to represent zones of climate. She learns the word 'temperate'.

At Easter Miss Blackthwaite gives each child a small Easter egg *from her own money*! This makes her wildly popular.

But Jill hates the sewing she now has to do, hates it with a passion as strong as anything she has yet felt. They have to sew hems on unbleached linen. First of all you have to make the bag to put the sewing in. Jill tacks her seams and then uses red and yellow thread to do wavy stitches, but the thread is always coming out of the eye of the needle. As long as she is in Standard One she will not finish the bag, never mind the further articles to be put in it. They call it 'Needlework', and boys do not have to do it but can go and garden instead, or make book-jackets. At first Jill prays her sewing will improve, but then she stops trying, tells herself she does not care.

A new school is not such a big change for Jill as living for nearly a year at Holm Garth. Auntie May is there all the time and Jill seems to see less of Mother. It feels sometimes as though Mother is not *there*. Jill and Nancy share a bed to begin with in the Ell room which is called Ell because of its shape. There are four big bedrooms on the first floor, and two attic bedrooms above them with a coloured skylight on the roof above the stairs. The maid once slept in the larger of the attics in the days when Grandpa was richer and had a big Morris car, because textiles were doing well.

While they are still living at Holm Garth waiting for their new house to be built, a Big Treat happens: Jill and Nancy are invited to a grand party in the White Swan Hotel in the town by two girls whose parents have got together for this purpose.

Auntie has reported that Joy and Ann will be going to it in 'party cloaks' of velvet and that it would be nice if she too could have a cloak. Auntie has a beautiful emerald cloak left over from the days when she went to dances, and they decide to cut it down for Jill. Nancy is decreed to be 'too young' for a cloak. The other problem is shoes. Joy and Ann are reported to possess gold sandals, so Jill and Nancy are provided with the next best thing, silver ballet shoes.

The taxi comes to collect all four girls since Joy and Ann live very near. Jill's lovely green cloak – of *real* velvet she is assured – is somehow longer and less swirly than the other girls'. Joy has a dark crimson cloak and Ann one of royal blue. Jill has imagined they will keep them on for the party – but no, each girl takes off her cloak on arrival and changes into her special party shoes. The ballroom is crowded with children, boys as well as girls, and quite a few ladies, including Ann's mother and aunt. It is very, very noisy.

There are several games that involve rushing round in circles and in one of these a big naughty boy trips Jill up after bashing her shin with his shoe. The pain is dreadful but she picks herself up and finds Ann's Auntie and another lady bending over her. 'Does it hurt? Come and sit down. There, there . . .' Jill is determined not to cry though she would like to. She tosses her hair, says 'It's all right' and limps back into the circle. The circle sweeps round and round to the music and Jill's leg hurts more and more. Every time she passes the two aunties she sees them looking at her mournfully and tut-tutting, shaking their heads. Finally the music stops and she is out again and makes her way to the chairs set round the room where Nancy is already sitting.

'Poor little thing,' she hears behind her and knows it is Ann's auntie but she is not going to acknowledge her.

'She's very *small* isn't she?' says another lady.

'But they say she's very *clever*,' replies the other.

Jill rushes away, determined not to be caught by their kindness. At that moment she hates the party and hates Mick Ormondroyd, who kicked her, most of all.

Mick Ormondroyd gets the prize for staying longest in Musical Chairs. He would! She thinks, he is just the sort of boy who says: 'Are we forced?' if ever asked to do anything.

Then it is time for ices and lemonade and at this all her deep anxieties return. Mother has specially asked her not to overeat and to see that Nancy does not overeat either. She must always look after Nancy.

'You're not to have an ice-cream *and* a lemonade,' Jill tells her patiently waiting sister as they are herded up to the table. 'Only one, not both. I don't want you to be sick.'

'I'm *never* sick,' says Nancy truthfully.

Jill chooses a lemonade with a straw but refuses the lovely ice-cream on its silver dish.

'Aren't you hungry, dear?' asks Ann's auntie.

'No, thank you. I don't eat ices', says Jill. 'But Nancy can have an ice-cream if she doesn't have a lemonade.' The auntie looks puzzled. 'Is your leg still hurting?' she asks.

'No – it's better,' lies Jill.

Nancy has seized a lemonade and is sucking it up quickly with her eye on an ice-cream. Jill feels desperate.

'You're not allowed both! I told you. I promised Mummy.'

But Nancy darts away and Jill sees her grab an ice-cream from another table. *She* does not, though. She sucks up her lemonade slowly – it is not fizzy – and comforts herself that she has tried to do what she promised, and although a big bruise is spreading in a lump on her shin, she does *not* feel sick.

Nancy is not sick either. It isn't fair. Still, Nancy hasn't a party cloak.

Unfortunately, a fortnight after this great event both girls come up in a horrible red rash and feel quite dreadful. It is measles and it has obviously been caught at the White Swan party. Jill wonders what she is being punished for, but the fire in her bedroom grate and the cosy convalescence make her feel comfortable. It is Nancy who gets bad earache as a result of the measles.

In the summer all the children must have an injection against diphtheria and then a Schick test to see if it has 'taken'. Jill's arm swells up and then she gets a very sore throat and has to go back to the big bedroom where she lay earlier with measles. Auntie May is very kind and sits up with her when she is delirious. Fortunately it does not turn out to be diphtheria but she knows that the grown-ups are frightened. The illness leads to her possessing something called a 'heart murmur'.

It is gratifying however very soon after this to be given a Coronation mug and a silver spoon, *twice*, both for Edward VIII and George VI.

After this year she is less and less often sick. True, parties and treats are always better being looked forward to or remembered than actually experienced. Putting on turquoise velvet dresses by the gas fire in Mother's bedroom; choosing 'prizes' of glass necklaces if you are actually giving the party – are all more fun than stamping round to Musical Parcel or doing Postman's Knock. Still, perhaps that is the point.

As with *Cinderella* you can always look back on the bits you enjoyed most.

In September they will move to their new house, but will still call at least twice a week at Holm Garth to see Granny and Grandpa and Aunt May. It is so peaceful there and Jill is allowed to go up to the Ell room and rummage in the big white drawer at the bottom of the double wardrobe where Granny and Auntie keep old photographs. The smell of that drawer is wonderful, the smell of the past: old sepia snaps and grander Cabinet photographs, in boxes and albums. She asks Auntie May about the people whose pictures are upstairs, and Auntie May likes nothing better than drawing Family Trees and telling her about her own grandparents, and about Aunt Topsy and Cousin Laura who are Granny Brook's mother's and father's relations. Some of the people in the photographs died young; there are many dead young men and women hanging from the branches of Auntie's trees, even dead children like little blossoms who have never opened.

Downstairs Grandpa may be listening to the football results on his big wireless and Jill will hear the names Bromwich Albion and Sheffield Wednesday, and Aston Villa, and wonder where they are. As well as the National Programme the wireless has strange stations marked on it: Droitwich and Beromünster and Luxembourg.

Once, Jill says to her aunt, who is also her godmother, 'It's sad you have no children, Auntie,' and Auntie May says 'I've got a bit of you,' and gives her a squeeze.

Jill always lingers at Holm Garth as long as she can, loving everything there from the red and green and orange pattern on the hall windows to the shiny mahogany pianola waiting to be played in the drawing room. At Christmas that room is full of the smell of cigars, wafting from behind the red velvet curtain that hangs over the door. Especially if some of the great uncles visit.

At Holm Garth there are coal fires with low grates even in the bedrooms. Auntie May lights fires in the morning with 'snails' of screwed-up paper she winds round a stick. In the dining room there is a high sideboard, and leather armchairs with fringes hanging from gold studs, and the picture of a fierce lion. In the sideboard there are tiny drawers with secrets. One of them has a store of toffee which you have to break into mouth-sized portions with a silver hammer. There is the large warm kitchen too where they often eat when Jill lives there, and where she sits on a scrubbed white stool. The kitchen is the place where she ate her porridge for breakfast the day Nancy was born. That porridge was runnier than Mother's, and was in the bowl where Boy Blue lurked, to be revealed only when the porridge oats were all eaten up – or pushed to the side – his blue jacket and yellow hair waiting for the spoon to reveal him. The same boy as in the nursery rhyme book where he lay asleep on his back in the picture, half propped up against a yellow haycock, in his hand a little horn. A sheep, probably one of Bo Peep's, is nibbling the hay to his right and in the distance several farmers and a cow are advancing. Boy Blue is part of summer.

Jill has known the house all her life, but living in it was different from visiting it or even staying for a few days. Auntie May missed her and Nancy when they left for their new house, but she went on helping to keep house for her parents, playing the piano, doing 'Barbola' work and singing in the Amateur Operatic Society. In her treasure boxes in her white bedroom, the pretty necklaces and rings are there for inspection when they visit. In the garden there is a rustic bench and in the summer deck chairs with canopies on the lawn, and a garden shed at the back with the heavenly smell of warm creosote, and another lawn, smothered in daisies.

At Holm Garth in the Ell Room there hangs that picture called *The Laughing Cavalier*. Why is he not what he seems, a cheerful man in a big hat whose glinting eyes follow you round the room? Because his eyes, at first merry, become threatening, will not leave your face. Wherever you turn, you see him looking at you so that you are forced against your will to look back at him, even from underneath the bedclothes. Jill dares not confess how he goes on frightening her, for if when she was two, staying over at Granny's and sleeping in the Ell Room bed, people were amused; at six or seven they think it is babyish. How can such a cheerful picture be sinister? they ask her.

Only Auntie May understands and turns his face to the wall. If he can't see her it is all right. Jill is quite happy for him to have to stare at the white wall. He is not a picture but a real man, a man who has power over her because, although she is frightened of him, he fascinates her and she can feel his will tugging at hers. The Laughing Cavalier is sure of himself. She knows he can wait for ever, to kill her. He is even more sinister than the Pig or the Bath, more like the House or the Leg, waiting ready to surprise her.

Other objects finally displace him and once more they hint at sudden death or death by fright. There is the abominable slide in the children's part of the park, but that can slowly be mastered and somehow accommodated, though the terror of climbing to the top is never repaid by the sudden swoosh downwards. Much worse is the Coronation Helter Skelter, one of the great treats of Coronation Year when all the children are taken in a 'charabang' to the local Pleasure Gardens. This is much worse because it is much higher and you have to go down on a mat. Jill has seen it once before, so knows what to expect and does not like what she knows. When therefore the charabanc hoots outside Holm Garth, waiting for her to join the happy throng, she suddenly clings to Auntie May and wails she does not want to go. No, please, need she go? Can't she stay at home? Nobody understands why and Jill dares not tell them, for, worse than tears and clinging, is for the other children to know she is afraid. But they take her on in the end, with all her fears of falling, and she manages to stay on the low swings and to wander round the Pleasure Gardens, never joining the queue for the high instrument of torture. Ever since she fell down the stairs when she was two and dented her forehead on the dolls' pram in the hall, she has feared losing her step. If you get to the top of the Helter Skelter you may fall, even be killed: you will certainly be hurt. Yet this is not the real fear. The fear is just of being high with nothing to hold on to. Especially when you have to negotiate a coconut mat at the top, on which you come down. The other children do it with whoops of glee.

In the baths you can drown; the Pig might eat you up, the Dead Leg chase you, the Laughing Cavalier wait for you, but it is the feeling round the fear that is worse than the possible outcome. Not just death, or falling, or drowning, but the dread.

'Cowardy, cowardy custard,' the other children cry, and she feels they are right to call her this. There is something wrong with her that she cannot enjoy these pleasures and fears to let herself go.

Other children though can also be frightened of things. The Bogey Man is often mentioned, perhaps the same one who had hidden in the folds of Daddy's old dressing-gown and lived in the loft, reached by the plain trap door, above the landing at the First House,

At Holm Garth there is an inner door in the attic wall and what Jill can't understand is that you are already *in* the attic, which is in the roof, so why do you need *another* door in the roof? It is exciting as well as frightening to climb the attic stairs to Lizzie the maid's old room and to find this door in the wall, a door that is never opened and which, Jill feels sure, leads to another 'secret' room.

Many stories are invented about this mysterious door, almost as many as have their origin in the wardrobe which opens at dead of night – so Jill tells Nancy – the door that allows the spirit of their great great grandfather to come out... There is something about attics, however, that is more mysterious than wardrobes. A bit like a secret garden, something no one else really knows about, where you can be alone. The attic itself, and the box room next to it, piled with hatboxes and old trunks, is not really frightening.

Perhaps Sarsama, the female, grown-up, very managing, occasionally scolding, competent and slightly sinister Sarsama who lived in the attic of the First House. was invented to frighten away the Bogey man? Sarsama had not come to live with them when they moved to Holm Garth. She stayed in the First House. So did Dih-Doh-Doh, for they were always together, vying with each other over the products of their baking day, endlessly discussing the day's doings and indulging in all-night marathon cooking bouts.

Neither did the stagnant weed-covered pond come along with them, nor the drooling idiot boy in the farmyard, nor the house with no windows. They belong to an earlier, simpler time of walks with Mother and Nancy.

Holm Garth has many interesting objects as well as the magic pianola: the machine that makes cream for example, the gilt framed portrait of great great grandfather in the oak-panelled hall, the big table in the dining room, under which you can hide. There are books – not as many as at home – but there is *The Moonstone* with its frontispiece of the man stealing the jewel with someone standing behind him, a man in a turban. This is very frightening since the man is hiding and the other man does not know he is there. The last things Jill catches sight of before she goes to sleep must not be this picture. If it is, she will die in the night...

Jill hates surprises, even the time when she was four and they had hidden a doll's pram in the hall. She had opened her Christmas presents in the bedroom and tried to pretend she didn't mind not getting the pram she had asked for. Then they had taken her by the hand to go downstairs and she had caught sight of the pram through the banisters, standing near the portrait. It was lovely, but it was a terrible shock, just when she had got used to the idea of *not* having one and had told the doll Barbara in her arms not to worry.

As the months pass, and Jill goes to her new school, the fears become less attached to objects, more to certain feelings. Her great fear at school is of being told off for being late for afternoon school which she frequently is. Somehow she can never resist staring in at Mr Sutcliffe's sweet-shop where he has arranged his big jars of Kali. Or she will lose something and waste time looking for it. Miss Blackthwaite will wearily reprove her for being late yet again and this will be followed by a reproof from Miss K for getting her sewing all wrong. Jill is also angry at herself because she can't stop the horrid needle from pricking her finger. She does not enjoy being reprimanded, particularly when she has already admonished herself for having so little patience.

She still dreads being found out, particularly by Mother, from whose purse she has more than once extracted a halfpenny to buy Kali. She has such a craving for sugar and such a sense of injustice at having less pocket money than some of her friends. The fear of being found out will eventually stop her pilfering further pennies. She will wheedle them out of Grandpa instead.

But once they arrive in the new house in the September after the Coronation, Mother decides that Nancy is ready for school. Nancy has pestered to go along with Jill but, not yet five, is put with the Babies. The Babies and Standard One do needlework together and for the first time Jill finds her sister useful, for Nancy will secretly take Jill's botched stitches, pull them out and do them again as well as finishing her own. No one expects Nancy to be able to sew, yet she can, and really well.

Jill is humbled.

NINE

The Cobbler

By the time she is with Miss K in Standard Two of the New School Jill has mastered the fairy cycle, though it has taken over a year. She is given one for Christmas. She often goes now for a swing in the park on the way back from Holm Garth, avoiding the 'rant' where rough boys send you up too high on the bench with its iron handles until she is sure it will crash.

In Standard Two they learn poetry as well as copper-plate writing. Miss K has them all reciting poems together:

Slowly, silently, now the moon,
Walks the night in her silver shoon...

There are poems too for Empire Day and a poem for every month of the year. Miss K reads them many stories too, and there are little story-books in her cupboard for good readers. One rainy playtime Jill reads one about a goldfish who falls down a drain. She is reminded of the 'Dead Leg' and the dead cat in the gutter, but it is all right for fish, since drains are full of water and this fish swims back to the sea – and anyway she is no longer frightened of the sort of things that used to terrify her.

Miss K asks them to write out a poem about the spring in their best handwriting and then to paint a border round it to give parents as an Easter present. Green and yellow next to each other are now Jill's favourite colours. There is something both magical and strange about those two colours together. She no longer likes blue; it is too 'ordinary'. Pale green and pale yellow give her a feeling she cannot describe.

In the new house the bathroom tiles are a bluey-green, a green not found in her paint-box, nearer the sheen and glamour of Christmas baubles or the traffic light 'Go'. The joy of colours overcomes her; there are so many, you can never encompass them all, and her artistic efforts are disappointing. Nothing she can paint comes close to the magic of her feelings. She tries words, which have a magic of their own; sometimes one word is enough to arouse the feelings, but if you put the words together they have to make sense, and their beauty evaporates.

Some words evoke more than the things they stand for, and suggest the feelings that surround them. Even the scent of chrysanthemums is connected to the word, just as the sharp silver of crystal is in the shape of the word on the page, like the crystals of the necklaces her mother gives Jill's friends at her seventh birthday party.

Their new house is very different from Holm Garth, newer and smaller. Jill goes through her new 'bottom drawer' of toys.

The Crystal Ball reminds her with vexed gratitude of Learie when she is next offered a present by a grown-up man. This time he is a cobbler and he lives down the road from her new house in a little shack which he locks up at night. She has entered upon a passionate phase of collecting matchboxes to make dolls' house furniture and other things. The Swan Vesta boxes are larger and more useful than the others, though she collects both the big and the small. The small boxes carry the legend 'Pilot Matches' and have a picture in red and blue of a man in a sou'wester. She never has enough money to buy her own boxes as the small ones are ½*d* and the large ones one penny each, and anyway matches are not allowed children, so she begs them from her father and mother. She spends hours laboriously sticking them together with Gloy and painting the finished products – beds and chests of drawers, with drawing-pins for knobs. A shoe-box is too big for the purpose, so it becomes a furniture repository or a real doll's bed. At Methodist Sunday School when she was very young they had used to make synagogues from shoe-boxes, with flat roofs and plasticine-based palm trees, but Jill had not been very good at it. She preferred to sing 'If I were a little twinkling star' with its sad tune – which she liked better than 'Jesus bids us shine'. Dolls'-house furniture is much easier than synagogues. Some girls make furniture from conkers and pins, but Jill's conkers usually split.

She happens to mention to the cobbler that she collects matchboxes, on one of her visits to him with a pair of Mother's shoes. On his little counter lies an empty Swan Vestas box. 'You can have it!' he says casually and she cannot believe her luck, for the cobbler smokes a pipe when he is not cobbling and therefore gets through rather a large quantity of matches. The cobbler is munificent and begins to keep back all his empty matchboxes for her so that she does not even have to take him a pair of shoes in exchange. It is almost too much; he says it is no trouble and he is glad she can find a use for them.

One day she counts eighty empty boxes. She has saved them for a gigantic 'jewel box' for the dolls Barbara and Sylvia, a piece of furniture to be stuck together then papered over and painted, ten inches high and eight inches across. As it is Sunday afternoon the shoemaker will have gone home. He must have a home for he locks the shack behind him every evening at six o'clock.

It is early autumn and the family has decided to go for a walk in the woods, about a mile away at their nearest point. On the way back they pick up Joan and Dorothy Jeffcock who are playing on the golf links. Jill rushes on ahead with them. She is wearing her best, most valuable, sparkling diamond ring that had appeared the Christmas before in a 'jewel cracker'. The ring has a large stone with 'filigree' claws round it and is absolutely beautiful. Usually she tucks her middle finger with the ring on it inwards and holds her hand inside the pocket of her blazer, but running along with Joan and Dorothy she has flung her hand out and suddenly she sees that the ring is not on it.

Desperately she begins to search along the grass verge – how long since it has been flung away? She dares not report the loss to her mother who is never sympathetic, always cross about her continual loss of possessions. Jill keeps thinking she sees it, sparkling in the grass, but it is hopeless. It has gone for ever! She does not cry, as that would be proof of guilt, but confides in Dorothy who says, 'Where? Where?' in a silly way for if she knew where, it would not be lost. When they get home for tea she feels empty and angry. Even the contemplated jewel box doesn't console. She remembers the penny she lost long ago.

The next day, however, although she still feels depressed, she decides to go to Tom the Cobbler after school for another matchbox, then, if there is time, to go back alone on the golf links' verge to search again. School seems to go on for ever. Monday is Needlework afternoon, a lesson to be dreaded. Once you are no longer in Standard One you are expected to learn neat stitches and make useful objects. There is a world of difference between making dolls' jewel chests and sewing unbleached linen with tiny stitches. Nancy, who is still in the Babies' class, can no longer do her stitching for her if she sits nearby.

At last the big hand-bell clanks away in the boys' playground and the prisoners escape. Jill goes straight down the road to Tom's shack and her spirits begin to rise. The lost diamond is still lying like a lump of undigested food in her stomach, making her heart beat wildly, but no one knows (except Dorothy) and she will just have to bear it alone.

She pushes open Tom's door. His machine is not whirring, which means he is having a chat with a customer. But what is this? The large form of PC Bennett sitting on the customer's chair and Tom is standing in an embarrassed way.

'Hello – come for your matchboxes?' he says and winks.

'What's this, now?' booms the constable, looking at Jill. Her heart sinks again. Giving matchboxes to children must be against the law? Tom will probably be fined – and she will be told off.

'They're only empty ones,' says Tom, looking, she thinks, a little alarmed. 'She comes for them regular, don't you, Jill? Here you are, love – a nice Vestas for you!'

'Oh, please – it's all right – I don't want it – not if...'

'And what are you going to do with that?' asks PC Bennett jovially.

'I make dolls' furniture.'

Now, she should ask him about the ring. Lost Property. It might be handed in? But she dared not. He looks menacing. Tom looks surprised when she says: 'But I've got lots now – really – I don't need any more.'

They are both turning towards each other with a sort of wink. She decides to escape. 'It's all right. I must go.' And she flees.

Somehow she retains the image of the policeman looking amused, but Tom looking rather annoyed.

Later, much later, Mum says: 'Do you still go to visit the cobbler for your matchboxes?'

'No,' Jill replies shortly.

A ring like Jill's turns up in the winter on Joan Jeffcock's finger, but Jill cannot be sure if it really is hers.

Somehow the big glass bulb that had been so useless, though beautiful, and the matchboxes that had been so useful but somehow *wrong* for her to have, get confused in Jill's mind. She still goes on losing her possessions, though some she gives away, including a dolls' jewel case to Dorothy Jeffcock.

'Have it. I'm too old to play with dolls now,' she says.

She avoids seeing Tom the Cobbler's hurt feelings ever after. Dad takes his shoes there for himself.

TEN

Little Boys and Dream Queens

Jill still both likes and fears little boys – likes some and fears others. All the children in the new houses play together every evening. Playing marbles with John and Edward at the old house long ago has changed into tagging along with boys who collect wood to burn on Bonfire night. It is called chumping, and she will help to make the Guy. There is much exploring of the 'Top Buildings' where the houses are yet only foundations with a few brick walls, though they don't find much wood there.

Boys don't join in girls' games much and never play with skipping ropes. That's for girls with their skipping games.

The boys prefer tree-climbing and birds-nesting and roaming around on bicycles in gangs. In the winter they play football and Jill is very proud if she is allowed to play with them now and again. She forms her own gang and calls herself Robin Hood and some of the boys tag along with Jill and her girl friends until they get bored, but they are very good at making bows from large garden canes, using pea-sticks for arrows.

Jill's nickname is 'Candy Tuft', a name given to her by two boys who swoop round the village on their bikes making nuisances of themselves. She is quite pleased to have this nickname. At least it means they have noticed her, and it is better than 'Brainbox' or 'Matchsticks'.

She has never seen a boy undressed, except for her small cousin John who does not count, as he was only a baby when she saw him. Even then she was both fascinated and repelled by his naked form kicking in his pram. It was very odd, what he had between his legs. There seemed to be three bits, or at least two, and they were a reddish purple. She cannot linger long enough to study the sight properly – and his nappy is soon on again. Another small boy does, however, add a surreptitious thrill to the Buildings Gang as it is his great pride to pee in a rainbow arc from the first floor (as yet unroofed) to the ground floor. Jill tells him mysteriously that girls cannot do this. He reports this to his mother who comes rushing round to Jill's mother to see what else she has been telling him.

Jill is casual: 'Oh, I just mentioned it – he wanted me to do it too,' she half fibs.

Some boys are very nice as friends, but Jill does not find them very exciting. Excitement and romance come quite another way, come out of the blue, repeatedly from the very first day at school till almost the last, from school and Sunday School, from the Missionary Society and the Brownies, in a succession of mysterious and beautiful females to whom she gives her heart and calls her Dream Queens.

Night after night she lies in bed sending herself through adventures, placing herself on an endless stage directing a spotlight of love towards the Queen of the moment, saving her from various fates – fires, and floods, and icy ponds.

When she was five there had been Miss Jackson of course, and little Miss King, at St Cedd's, the First School. Young curly-haired Miss King had not really counted because she was not quite mysterious enough. She was kind and pretty, and Jill had taken advantage of her and called her Miss Queen, and been admonished for rudeness. Miss Jackson had been different – older than Miss King, dark and angular with a sallow complexion and an embarrassed manner. At dinner time she had used to take Jill to the bus-stop to ride the three stops home where Mother was waiting to collect her. One day they were on their way to the bus when Miss Jackson slipped in a puddle and went down. Jill had seen a flash of pink knicker and petticoat which she immediately pretended she had *not* seen, for Miss Jackson seemed to be quite ashamed of herself. 'Rescuing Miss Jackson', a long story involving a broken ankle, was the result of this adventure and had kept Jill happily awake every evening. But alas, her dear Miss Jackson slipped away from her life for ever when she decided to love Miss Blackthwaite.

She realises that Miss Blackthwaite is not a beauty, but she seems sad, or Jill likes to imagine this is the case. Miss Blackthwaite takes out her tuning fork for their tonic Sol-Faa and the class sings the 'Doh' and then attempts to sing the note pointed to on the chart by Miss Blackthwaite's long stick.

Jill always waits for the Fah-Me-Ray. There is something inexpressibly sad about this interval, something that goes with leaves falling in autumn, and with remembering things. When they sing it, Jill imagines that Miss Blackthwaite's lover is waiting for her to carry her 'over the hills and far away'. She sees him as a prince who loves the teacher with yearning, and imagines Miss Blackthwaite thinking of him as the class sing these three notes. She feels Miss Blackthwaite to be a melancholy person, and stares at her sympathetically during the daily 'Now the day is over', her favourite hymn, which has to bear a good deal of repetition, for they always sing it at the end of the day in autumn and winter. Not long after this Auntie May begins to teach her to play the piano, and she discovers notes and combinations of notes that are beautiful in themselves. And here is the old Fah-Me-Ray in the key of C! It is very sad, the same sadness as in 'Now the day is over'. But so much hard work is necessary if you are to learn to play tunes; words are easier.

Jill looks out of the window at the back where she sits, and somehow the sad tune becomes a part of herself and a part of the end of the day and the trees in the school garden and the rooks going back to the elms near the church and, later, a part of the grey pavement and the lamp coming on over the station bridge, and tea-time.

Miss Blackthwaite is part of all this as is the thought that year of the poor Chinese who are at war. Jill prays for them, as the year before she prayed for the Abyssinians when they were still at the First House. When the prayer is finished, Mother explains that the leader in that country, Haile Selassie, has fled to England. Soon there are to be more wars. Mother has always said Jill's prayers with her, and soon after her arrival at her new school Mother adds a prayer for Spain. Jill's prayers do not appear to have been answered by God since the war there goes on for a year or two after that. Mother reads about it in the newspaper.

Miss Blackthwaite is now in Jill's prayers, and the imaginary lover who is perhaps a soldier. Miss Blackthwaite lasts for a long time in Jill's dreams, but there comes a time when the Headmaster announces she is to leave to look after her old parents across the Pennines. Jill is sure that this is not the real explanation. The Fah-Me-Ray is poignant in their last music lesson and Jill has a lump in her throat. It is, though, pleasurably sad to think of the teacher far away at last, but difficult to fit this fact into her fantasies.

For a time she has to be content with old dreams, for the next two teachers in Standard Two and Three do not easily lend themselves to the heroic or the magical or even the sentimental. Even so, with little to go on, Jill bravely rescues Miss Gaukroger from a fire and from a lake on which she has been skating when the ice breaks. Miss Gaukroger is rather old for all this, and Jill is not very satisfied. Rescue for her dreams is, however, at hand at Sunday School and at Brownies. The Sunday School has an offshoot in a Missionary Society for younger members which meets weekly, and one of the leaders is a small mysteriously sweet lady with a German name, Miss Büchsel.

Jill spends many happy hours listening to her soft voice

extolling the exploits of a woman missionary in darkest Africa and manages to hero-worship the missionary as well as her disciple. But somehow Miss Büchsel is too *good* – and like Miss Blackthwaite has an Aged Parent with whom she spends most of her time. The missionary then comes to speak to them, but she is disappointingly unglamorous, though Jill goes on heroine-worshipping her too for a time.

Brownies, though, is exciting when a new Brown Owl arrives, dark and beautiful and engaged to be married. She lives in one of the old eighteenth-century houses facing the school field and does not speak with the same accent as others in the village. By this time many refugees and evacuees are living in Jill's village and people are no longer praying for the Chinese or the Abyssinians but for themselves.

The Brownies see their role as part of the War Effort, knitting squares for blankets and learning knots which might be useful in the tying up of German prisoners. School is more exciting too if air-raid practices punctuate the lessons, and Jill worries more about leading the class off to the shelter when the bell goes for air-raid practice than about any actual air-raid. The children are then encouraged to sing raucous popular songs in the shelter.

Brown Owl seems a little distant from all this, but she is a sympathetic young woman who talks freely to the Brownies. To Rita Oldroyd Jill has said that she loves Brown Owl. Rita Oldroyd tells Brown Owl: 'Jill's overseen on you, Miss.'

Brown Owl, not acquainted with the dialect, smiles. Rita apparently pursues the matter for, the next week, Brown Owl says casually to Jill 'I heard something – is it true? – that you are cross with Tawny Owl?'

'Oh, no,' breathes Jill. 'I just said I would rather have *you*.' It is the first time she has ever mentioned her feelings to their object and she is both gleeful and embarrassed. Brown Owl seems to consider the matter, then smiles and says she is glad Jill enjoys her group.

It is a very happy time, picnicking in the long grass, skipping, singing and holding hands as they dance around.

All summer it lasts. But by autumn Jill is a little bored by Brownies, if not bored by her nightly escapades rescuing Brown Owl from the Germans or sacrificing herself that Brown Owl might live.

Brown Owl's father is called away to manage another bank and Brown Owl tells them she is getting married. He is a soldier. Jill is both excited and sorry. Brown Owl is happy and in love and in September she says goodbye to her little flock and goes off to her wedding. The house remains untenanted and the Brownies find difficulty in replacing her. Jill is happy that she has told her love. It all seems very satisfactory and she feels it has been found acceptable.

By the time she is nine Jill has begun to take more notice of some of the boys, to want to play football with them. Boys have dogs and still play with bows and arrows and fight with you until their mothers tell them it is 'not done' to fight girls. This always makes Jill angry; not all boys are strong and you surely ought to be allowed to fight them if you want? They do not frighten her any more. Even horrible 'Batty Albert Milton', who spills the ink on her compositions on purpose is more of a nuisance than a threat.

A year or two later, when Brownies have faded away and Brown Owl is a memory to be taken out and occasionally dusted and her face and features recalled, Rita Oldroyd is first with the news which she imparts solemnly and yet incredulously.

Brown Owl is dead!

Not having a baby – no, but the victim of a terrible disease.

Jill feels cold, betrayed. Is this how love ends? Can it be true? It was one of her happiest feelings and she feels it is cancelled out now for ever.

'But she knew I loved her!' she thinks as she weeps that night in her bed.

There are some things you cannot be rescued from. Later, when she is eleven at the Grammar School, she will fall passionately in love again, this time with Miss Dunfermline –

and remain in love with her until Miss Dunfermline leaves to get married.

Until she is sixteen she will go on falling in love with beautiful women.

ELEVEN

Phases and Pleasures

There had been a big oak desk at Holm Garth with an inside top where bottles of different coloured inks and steel nibs were to be found. Jill spent blissful hours there with paper and pen. She preferred the green ink. Long before they moved into their brand new house, only a mile or so away from the First House, Jill was writing poems which she showed to Father or Auntie May, who encouraged her. The poems were mostly about flowers and spring.

SPRING FLOWERS

I do like the primrose,
She is so fair.
And I like the violet too,
For she scents the air –
Then the daffodilly
Her dress is gay
She makes me think of other flowers,
At their frolicking play.
Then the sweet forget- me-not
I do just adore,

And bluebells too I love,
They carpet the woodland floor

By the time she acquired copperplate writing in Miss K's class, Miss Blackthwaite had left, and Jill had already exchanged big Holm Garth for the New House, built to Mother's specifications. They watched it grow at weekends from its foundations, the first of a loop of houses built where once were market-gardens.

She prefers to stay in and read but Mother turfs her and Nancy 'out to play'. She makes the best of it by founding a 'society' in emulation of the 'Treasure Seekers'. It is to be only the first of many societies and gangs, some of which will last years.

She buys two blue ha'penny exercise books in which to write her plays, which her friends are supposed to act, for the best parts are carefully assigned to Joan and Joyce, her present best friends. The plays are obliged to have large casts of minor characters to fit in the rest of the class, and their speeches are rather short, consisting mainly of saying 'Me too!' after every remark of the hero when he has decided to track down a burglar or put out a fire. The plays continue for a year or so.

Reading and writing are, however, not her only pleasures. The identification with Miss Blackthwaite's feelings, accompanied and urged on by music, is not to be the last time music infiltrates Jill's life of feeling, even to the extent of taking over the feeling.

Later, songs or tunes will evoke past emotions almost as poignantly as smells. At St Cedd's she had been overcome and haunted by the beauty of 'Harvest moon' and 'If I were a little twinkling star', and hymns continue to play an important part after Standard Two of the New School. Not only hymns. Back in the old Rhyl Terrace days she had listened to her father's precious wireless crooning out something about Alabama – the word was most soothing. 'Pennies from heaven' followed, a tune much whistled by Mr Taylor, and one which he tried to teach his budgerigars. Before the war, the tunes, she realises, were mostly about 'love'.

Other pleasures are not always connected with music. Great passions submerge her seasonally, and sometimes more frequently, passions she names 'phases'. They *are* like falling in love, and indeed they are falling in love, but more respectably than with a person. They are not cast off lightly either. Some return every year like Conkers and Snow and Christmas and Sledging and Wild Flowers and Leaf Collecting. Some come and go away seemingly for ever, like looking after babies, practising First Aid, and writing about infectious diseases. Others though stay for years, and some for ever.

There are the pleasures of taste and smell; the pleasures of collecting and learning; the pleasures of making and the pleasures of playing and imagining. She never seems to have been without them. Sometimes they are connected with places – like Rooks Nest in its private park, so near to them, or Sheepden Hall, the local Tudor house, that has become a museum; or the moors; or Haworth.

Sometimes the joys are linked to people in books, or people who write books, or with friends, or invented friends, or with walks and exploring, or with pretending she is a nurse or a teacher, or with places she has never seen and longs to see, or with past heroes and heroines.

Yet pleasures are not quite the same as 'phases', for 'phases' involve activity whereas pleasures can be purely passive, like smelling creosote or autumn bonfires or looking at dahlias and chrysanthemums in gardening catalogues, flowers which are somehow more beautiful – in a way she feels to be wrong – than the 'real' flowers. It is when you collect the pictures or the wild flowers or try to find words for the sensation the smell gives you that a 'phase' is round the corner.

For years she owns a cheap little book, published by the Co-operative Wholesale Society in which there are several paintings of bluebell woods, and cows in green fields which she thinks unsurpassingly lovely. Just as her cigarette card albums, particularly the Kings and Queens of England, and the photographs of the Beauty Spots of England, entrance her. The Valley of the Wye and the 'River Cherwell at Oxford' are never more beautiful in her mind than in these small pictures, speaking of an England she does not yet know. And the Kings and Queens, so many and all so different, golden romantic Richard Lionheart her favourite, and Elizabeth in her collar of pearls. She savours their names as she savours many names, and attaches them to imaginary children, or characters of her own creation.

Sensual pleasures have been most acute at a very early age – the taste of those early Swizzles that cost one halfpenny a packet, sharp-sweet on the tongue, and the sight of buttercups and daisies on her cotton dress; the orange and yellow and blue of the porridge plate at Holm Garth with Little Boy Blue asleep in the middle. Jill loved Little Boy Blue.

By the time she is eight she enjoys remembering. She remembers a winter day at the First House, and the red of the apple skin, the pure pinky-white of its inside that Kathleen had bitten into on the other side of the kitchen window, asking her out to play. She remembers the velvety brown hat she had worn on her first day at St Cedd's. They are things that go back to her very beginnings and will be as sharply recalled as the taste of a Fisherman's Friend, the little black sweet Margaret's mother gave her one cold morning when she went to call for Margaret to go to school.

Very early Christmases possessed the same magic: the carrot on the dish for the reindeer in the Hall at Granny's, and Auntie's little tree with the silver and green glass ornaments. Putting the holly up on Christmas Eve when another Aunt called with a present, and everyone was happy. Spending pocket-money in the old market – delightful things like dolls' hot-water bottles and feeding bottles and practical jokes and Lucky Bags and gobstoppers...

The feeling of there being so much of everything came from the market and never left her. She was greedy, had to learn to look, not have. The same feeling would come in the Bluebell

Wood and by the bramble bushes. Thousands and thousands of bluebells; hundreds and hundreds of ripe blackberries – better gloated over than picked or eaten.

The library makes her feel the same, but here she can have it all, bit by bit. The difficulty is in choosing when you can take only one book home. The first library book she ever chooses for herself is *The Invisible Prince* by Andrew Lang. She is disappointed by it and goes back to *Little Women*. Then she visits the library again and discovers a writer called E Nesbit in a fat orange edition. There are several books by this person and she tears into them all, discovers 'The Wonderful Garden' and the language of flowers. 'Caroline, Charlotte and Charles', she intones.

They are special names; she thinks of calling her dolls by them but the dolls obstinately remain Rosemary, Barbara, and Sally the baby doll.

Names, though, are a problem. The first plays, written in those little blue notebooks included as many names as she might cram into the action – starting with her friends, Joan and Joyce and Jean, and the boys – George, Frank, David and John. Family history would provide more; this time, Emmas and Elizas and Benjamins. Names become a new 'phase'; hours are spent tracing back family lines to a past she has not dreamt of but which she must now account for by herself. Aunt May is a mine of information.

Jill finds the same thrill in painting, using all the colours in the paint box because she likes their names. Rose Madder is an Irish schoolgirl with dark hair and blue eyes; Gamboge is a ginger frizzy woman who kept a shop; Green Bice is a nasty spinster and Vermilion a spoilt boy. Burnt Sienna and Burnt Umber are spirits of the bonfire, and Prussian Blue and Ultramarine and Emerald are aristocrats.

She and Nancy are given some parchment paper and many old Christmas cards to make calendars and 'new' cards. Making them, painting the cards, making brooches from open empty hazelnut shells, toiling over items for the Chapel Sale of Work, takes up much time. Chapel is behind a great deal of juvenile activity, not only in the missionary field and connected with the Sunday School rituals, but also in encouraging the beauty of language. The language of the Church of England, and therefore of the Religious Instruction at school, is even more exciting: *Immortal, Invisible ... casting down their golden crowns upon the glassy sea ... the pomps and vanity of this wicked world... Life everlasting...*

Organised 'pleasures' differ from the active 'phases' which Jill continues to catch, like measles. Seasons and weather are the background against which she and Nancy pursue their enthusiasms. For a whole autumn they collect leaves and stick them into a thick ledger. Jill decorates each page with a curly copperplate name, hoping she's got it right. Rowan and hornbeam and hawthorn are special; oak and elm, sycamore, beech and ash more ordinary. The satisfaction of pinning them down does not last long, for there are some whose names she cannot find and she is not very good at recognising the real ones from the book. She gives up and comforts herself with the thought that *some* book will have them all. The world is so full!

'First Finds' at school happen every spring: wild flowers are collected on family walks – celandines and kingcups, windflowers, milkmaids, rare cowslips, coltsfoot, shepherd's purse, vetch, clover and wild strawberries, harebells, primroses. The school gives her a gold star but the flowers fade and do not seem the same pressed in blotting-paper.

At Holm Garth she had played with her Teacher's Box, with its sum cards and notebooks, pencils, rubbers and dip-in pens. She had invented a class of children and given them all marks. But after that there was nothing much else to do except make up spelling tests. She had written her first stories about giants and fairies and greedy children in her stiff-backed black book. Her first story had happened first of all in her head, when she was five. It was called 'The Giant Who Was Lazy' and was about a giant who could never get up in the morning until he swallowed an alarm clock. Then he could, for he had 'the time inside him'. Other poems had followed upon 'I do like the primrose', poems in which she sought for rhymes for flowers (showers), fair (air), day (gay)... More stories, more poems were to come.

The Teacher's Box is finally abandoned when the Silver Pin Society is formed.

Pins are easy to obtain for badges. Jill's first 'society' has a long constitution and is limited to a handful of friends. Its main function is to be and to remain a secret, and its second function is that of demanding loyalty to itself. It is followed later at decent intervals by the Swan Club, the Smugglers' Adventure Gang and the Literary and Dramatic Society.

TWELVE

Nine Years Old

The first summer in the new house had been an exciting one, with rumours of war, not far away in Spain or Abyssinia, but in *England*. Men went about digging shelters and stacking sand-bags. Children had to go to the branch library in the next village to be fitted with gas-masks, horrible sweaty contraptions stored in square cardboard boxes. It was odd going to the library and coming back not with books but with these objects. But Jill no longer feared 'shapes' and was already a frequent visitor to the library room at the top of the stairs in the building where the old Council offices used to be. It was not as big or grand as the town library where she used to go with her father. That library smelt of dust and polish; this branch library was more friendly.

War did not come that summer but the next.

Jill hated change, and when she was almost nine things happened to make her aware that life is always changing: nothing stays for ever.

When he was sixty-six Grandpa Brook had been knocked down by a bicycle. He had also been suffering from bronchitis, which the shock waves from his accident made worse. Yet he did not die of these things but from a cerebral haemorrhage early one Saturday morning at the end of August in the following year, exactly one week before the outbreak of the war he had predicted would never come to pass.

A few days after his funeral, England was at war.

Jill is sent out to play with Nancy on the morning Grandpa dies. They feel self-important. They go to the swings and tell a friend, a boy who plays with them:

'Our grandfather has died.'

'What is that?' asks John who is only five.

Jill and Nancy do not go to Grandpa's funeral in the great 'necropolis' at Woolsford where Great Grandpa Brook and Great Great Grandpa Brook now lie with their wives. No, they are dispatched for the afternoon to their other grandparents.

Nanny Wood takes them to the Bowling Green to take their minds off Grandpa Brook, for whom they have wept for days, surprising their mother. Has she not realised how much she and Nancy loved him?

Everything is wrong: death, and not enough money in the bank, and war. There is a visit from a solicitor great uncle, another of Grandpa's brothers. He suggests that Auntie May will have to find work now, and she so dislikes teaching.

Granny Brook takes in a bank manager from London whose bank has been moved north. He is a kind man who gives Jill a beautiful doll called Trudy from the Austrian Tyrol, for he has visited Austria and Germany, though he has never seen Hitler.

The war will changes people's lives. Things eventually calm down a little, after the arrival of the first wave of 'evacuees'. Now no longer are hours of school-time spent singing in the air-raid shelter, but gas-masks are still a reality and must be taken to school every day. Only when Eileen, an evacuee from Poplar, describes to her how her uncle was dug out dead from his bombed house, does Jill suddenly realise that it could have been her own uncle if they had lived nearer London. But she pushes this knowledge down, doesn't want to think about it. It is cowardly of her but she cannot bear it.

Jill is always hungry, stuffs herself with bread and treacle. Mother still opens tins of food from 'The Empire', the sort whose label Jill used to steam off carefully for Miss K's collection in the old pre-war days, but now food is rationed.

A few months after the war begins, Jill and her three best friends are put up a class to Standard Four. It is good for Jill. With girls and boys a year older she has to work a little harder to be among the first, or 'top', three in the class. All their marks are ritually added up every term – marks for composition and mental arithmetic and sums. In Standard Four you are expected to know how to do fractions. Standard Three has not been taught them, so Jill and Joan and Margaret and Marie stay in for a few playtimes while Peter and Doreen and Betty explain the addition and subtraction, multiplication and division of vulgar fractions. Jill enjoys this – applying a rule and seeing it come out right. Peter and Betty both want to be teachers, so they are good at explaining.

It is Jill's turn to explain when the Channel Islanders come to live in the town. Many of them cannot read, and so Jill and her friends are deputed to take small groups in a special classroom to try to help them.

'We ain't got time to read, Miss,' said one. 'It's the tomatoes – they keep you busy.'

The class teacher of Standard Four is Mr George, who is very soon to be called up. He has thick frizzy hair and thick glasses and his moods are very changeable. If he is on duty at playtime he encourages the girls to walk round the field chatting to him. Once back in the classroom however, when the chatting gets out of hand Mr George takes a gym shoe and 'slippers' the unruly.

Jill is a talkative child and cannot believe it when he calls her out one day after what must have been many repeated warnings. She must have been cheeky.

'Bend over!' he says.

It does not hurt; it is more the embarrassment and the feeling silly. How dare he slipper *her*? She resolves not to talk to him any more; some other girl can entertain him.

She tries after that to keep her mouth shut during lessons. Rather than chatting to her friends when she is bored she decides instead to write. Under the desk of course, in secret.

She has already written one or two small descriptions of glamorous ladies for her own delectation on scraps of wartime economy paper torn from a notebook. These have gone down well with friends so she goes on to write each girl a description of herself. They all seem pleased when they are read out by Jill in the playground:

A Description of the Fairy Queen

> She had on a gauzy bodice of silver and a pink crinoline of fine muslin. In her hair, which was golden, were a few fresh violets, the fragrance of which filled the ballroom. Her eyes were forget-me-not blue and her slippers were the colour of the new-born daisy. So do you not wonder that everyone in the ballroom was transfixed by the lovely sight?

This Fairy Queen idea reminds her of a time when she was very very young and thought she saw Tinkerbell flying above the lamp in her bedroom. She saw another fairy long ago in Cinderella, and there have been countless fairies in stories ever since, but she stopped reading about them when she was about seven. Somehow real life is now more interesting. Jo March is not a fairy, nor Rebecca of Sunnybrook Farm. But for the girls she has resurrected the Fairy Queen.

Rosemarie the Fairest of All

Her lips were the colour of red roses and her teeth white as the whitest snow. On her hair was a silver tiara decorated with the brightest diamonds. Her arms were covered with gossamer mittens. She was clothed with a golden lace dress which shone brighter than any star. Her shoes were silver and her stockings were mauve and green. Her eyes were blue as the summer sky and her whole appearance was beautiful.

Sylvia of the Sapphires

Her garments were coloured with sapphires and diamonds which were studded in her hair. Her eyes were violet-blue and her lips as red as the roses in the garden. On her feet were slippers of satin covered with sapphires. On her arms – to add to her beauty – were bracelets of gold. Her hair was jet black.

'But there's nobody here called Sylvia,' objects Joan.

'No, well they were imaginary. But I've done Stella and Eileen. Here's one for you, Eileen:

Eileen the Exquisite

Her dress was of blue organdie studded with pearls. In her hands she carried a spray of lavender. Her hair was jet black, curled in ringlets that fell on her shoulders. On her hair was a circle of lavender. Her feet were covered in satin slippers studded with diamond studs. Her breath was like scented roses, which scent filled the ballroom.'

'What's mine say? asks Stella.

'Here you are:'

> On her hair were two beautiful stars that shone at each side of her jet black hair which curled gracefully on her shoulders. Her skin was a smooth olive and on her lovely arms was a golden bracelet studded with sapphires. Her dress was of purple taffeta and on her legs were silver costly stockings. On her feet were slippers of purple satin studded with emeralds that glittered in the June sunlight and shone with the splendour of a thousand stars.'

'Oh, it's lovely!' breathed Eileen.

Stella looked pensive.

'I'll do Margaret and Joan tomorrow,' promises Jill.

Osbert George has not been the only young man to whom she chats. Out of school there is their neighbour's son, Leslie, who is about seventeen or eighteen, and is also waiting to be called up. Leslie has a passion for cycling, and for his dog, a lovely golden collie called Prince.

Jill's only physical accomplishment is riding a bicycle, which she often does with friends, going as far as the woods beyond the next village. Leslie introduces her to the intricacies of mending a puncture, and together they sometimes cycle down the road to Mr Blagden's cycle shop. Jill's new bicycle is a 24-inch Hercules and she finds cycle lore fascinating. Together they look at shiny catalogues of larger models with 'three speed' like Leslie's, and cycle back in single file. Prince runs along by his master's side barking. There is little traffic on the roads, and only PC Bennett to keep a watchful eye on anyone who does not 'Halt at Major Road Ahead.'

Prince and Leslie give Jill the idea for another of her stories. She calls Leslie 'Jack 'and it is an adventure story. The heroic heroine, along with her friend Jack, helps a wounded airman who has fallen out of his aeroplane on to a convenient rock. She writes it all one Saturday afternoon and reads it to Leslie on the Monday.

He listens patiently and is very appreciative.

At home she often says, 'I wish we had a dog.'

Her mother says dogs are dirty and never get enough to eat.

'A cat then?'

But Mother once had a cat who had died young and says she couldn't bear to have another.

'That was ages ago – before you were married!'

After this they buy two goldfish, Freddie and Freda, but unfortunately Freda soon gobbles up Freddie.

Mother has little real love for animals. It is Father who likes them, just as he likes working in his garden, and enjoys going for walks in the country. He knows the names of birds and flowers and has built a bird table in the back garden. Mother does take an occasional interest in nature study and one day Mother and Father spend hours looking up Viper's Bugloss and Blue Bugle. A blue flower grows on the railway embankment but nobody appears to know which of the two it is.

Jill listens to *Children's Hour* on the wireless especially to 'Out with Romany'. She writes to him about the birds in their garden and receives a reply that she sticks in her autograph album.

But when the war comes, some of their flowers have to go. Father is Digging for Victory. Jill suspects he does not really enjoy all this digging.

One day he shows her a poem he has written about his Saturday afternoon task.

'It's a parody of Tennyson,' he explains, 'you know? –

Break, break, break,
On thy cold grey stones,
O sea!
And I would that my tongue could utter
The thoughts that arise in me!'

Jill does not know the poem but finds it in her father's

red-leather-bound *Collected Tennyson* that was given to him along with *Collected Pope* on his fifteenth birthday. Father's poem starts:

Dig dig dig in the cold grey earth O Men,
And I would that I could utter
The thoughts that arise now and then –

She thinks it very clever.

Jill loves reading poetry aloud. In a dusty cupboard at school she has discovered a book with Sir Henry Newbolt's 'The Fighting Temeraire' and Alfred Noyes's 'Sherwood'.

Alone, she repeats:

Now the sunset breezes shiver
And she's fading down the river
But in England's heart for ever
She's the *Fighting Temeraire.*

and

Softly over Sherwood the south wind blows
All the heart of England hid in every rose...

Oh if she could only write like that! Her heroes have long been Lord Nelson and Robin Hood, and the poems make them even more romantic.

Different feelings are drawn out of her by the words and music of 'Drink to me only with thine eyes' which she considers the most beautiful tune she has ever heard – until she hears 'Greensleeves' and reads the words that go with it. The song about Barbara Allen is more disturbing, cruel. There is something strange too about the woman called 'Senta' whose story from the Flying Dutchman a trainee teacher tells them, but she cannot quite put her finger on it.

But even non-love songs can have sad tunes. The chorus of

'The quartermaster's stores' seems to Jill very sad, though everyone else thinks it funny when the singer comes to 'My eyes are dim I cannot see'. The same with 'We're gonna hang out the washing on the Siegfried line'. That is a very sad song, she feels, and is proved correct. Other children prefer 'I've got sixpence', which always calls to mind the silver bit Granny gives her every Saturday, that has to be put into the Yorkshire Penny Bank or towards a National Savings Certificate.

All around them is the music of war. Simple, very popular songs. Jean Darley confesses in the shelter that 'Roll out the barrel' is the saddest and most beautiful tune she knows. Jill finds this a touching admission. 'Drink to me only with thine eyes' has a similar sound, she thinks.

Many of the songs, like the verses she has discovered, are about England. Every Wednesday there is a concert in the hall when the school assembles to sing patriotic and popular ditties. Here too those children who are 'learning the piano' are obliged to perform. 'Real' music is the waltz from the *Sleeping Beauty* that haunts Jill. She tries to play it on the piano in simplified form. It is even harder than 'Some day my prince will come'.

The songs the headmaster chooses for them to sing are not usually about love. He never gets round to 'All the things you are' or 'You are the only kiss of springtime' ... preferring 'London Pride', 'There'll always be an England', 'Run rabbit run', and 'Give a little whistle'. The children know all these songs from listening to the Forces Programme and *Workers' Playtime*, and both children and grown-ups sing and whistle them everywhere. There is 'I yi yi I like you very much' and 'Deep in the heart of Texas'; there is 'You are my sunshine'; 'You'd be so nice to come home to'; 'Mares eat oats and does eat oats and little lambs eat ivy'; 'Don't fence me in'; 'South of the border, down Mexico way'; 'Little Sir Echo'; 'Wish me luck as you wave me goodbye'; 'We'll meet again'; 'Kiss me goodnight Sergeant Major'; 'Let him go, let him tarry', and 'A nightingale sang in Berkeley Square'.

Much more exciting are 'Just one of those things'; 'Room

five hundred and four'; 'These foolish things remind me of you'; 'Smoke gets in your eyes' and 'As time goes by'.

Later in the war when the old school shelter practice is a distant memory, they will be singing 'We'll gather lilacs', 'When the lights go on again all over the world', and 'Lilli Marlene', whose German words Jill will commit to memory.

THIRTEEN

Sunday School

Jill had accompanied Joan long before the beginning of the war to Sunday School. When she lived at the First House she had attended the Methodist Sunday School where people – not Jill – had made synagogues out of plasticine, but the Sunday School she began to attend when she was seven or eight was a different one.

There is a harmonium in a little back room, for the building was once the Chapel, before the smart new Chapel with its spire was built seventy years ago. Sunbeams come through the window of this little room and catch motes of dust in swirling bands, reminding Jill of the upstairs rooms in the First House. It is peaceful in this room with its cupboards of old books that even *smell* of dust. Jill begs to borrow them.

In the main hall they assemble to sing hymns and listen to Bible stories before they disperse to classrooms where volunteers take small groups. Connected with this chapel are many flourishing clubs. For children there is the Junior Branch of the London Missionary Society – 'Pilots' – which meets every Wednesday and is extremely popular.

The people you go to Sunday School with are on the whole the same ones who sit next to you in the National School, unless your ordinary school friends happen to be Church of England, like the National School. 'Chapel' is more popular with children, who can belt out 'We've a story to tell to the nations' or gently croon 'Just as I am', or 'Sun of my soul'... They no longer sing Jill's old favourite hymn 'If I were a little twinkling star'; it is too babyish.

After morning Sunday School you go to Chapel but are allowed to leave early. You go to Sunday School again in the afternoon, and in winter you leave about sunset after singing 'The day thou gavest'. Sunday is a day when all the shops are shut and all the swings in the park locked: the Day of Rest. It is 'against the law' to swing on a Sunday. If you attend Sunday School regularly you get a prize; they give you books, usually about nature study. Jill covets the Wonder Books – large, shiny full of lore.

But Sunday School is sometimes tedious and Jill and her friend Joan perfect a stamp-swapping session as they sit on the benches together at the back. Joan is especially good at bringing trophies from her deceased grandfather's study. He was a philatelist, and Jill sees the precious British North Borneo stamps for the first time. Packets of stamps are sold in the town but they are of places that appear to exist only to produce highly ornamental stamps of great size, such as those of 'Tanna Tuva', which she can never find on the map. Together Joan and Jill plan what they will do with the thousands of pounds they will receive for their unique collection of these pale yellow British North Borneos, said to be 'rare' in the catalogue. Some find their way to Jill's album. Foreign stamps are a hobby, not exactly a phase. The war enters even this pastime when correspondents are sought from all the Allies who might provide stamps.

Sales of Work continue at Sunday School. 'French knitting' and 'raffia work' are popular, as well as ordinary knitting, which Jill can just about manage, and many are the pen-wipers, egg cosies, calendars, mats, needle books, and pin-cushions laboured over to sell at the children's stall. There are also Chapel concerts. At one of them a song is rendered by a dark young man with a beautiful voice. Jill falls in love with him too, but she never sees him again: he has come from another village. She also rather fancies one of the visiting preachers who has lovely eyes, but he only visits them once.

The Harvest Festival is the pinnacle of the year. Jill looks forward to it, because the fruits and the flowers are so beautiful, especially the dahlias and chrysanthemums. On one of those endless Saturday afternoons of early autumn people go to the Chapel, to arrange baskets of fruit and sheaves of flowers against green foliage, to make a purple and red and orange and yellow glow. They pile them all on the broad window sills and at the bottom of the Communion table: heaps of shining apples, crab-apples, pears, plums, yellowy-green marrows, bronze and yellow and white chrysanthemums, garish dahlias, ordinary Michaelmas daisies. Jill's favourite colour is now mauve. Even in the war, when there are no oranges or bananas, the colours of the home-grown fruit and flowers gleam in the dusk.

They look different, ordinary, when they are seen on Sunday morning.

FOURTEEN

Arthur

When a hard winter sets in there is less playing out, more music practice, the *Girls' Crystal* hidden behind the page of music on the stand. Jill finds she can learn the piece off by heart and play it mechanically while she reads the adventures of Noël, the private detective. She is half ashamed of herself for finding the *Girls' Crystal* so enthralling. Sometimes she has time for a good long read of the thick schoolgirl stories, on pages like blotting paper, lent by cousins who have grown up and bequeathed their twenties' fiction to the bookshelves of younger members of the family. If Mother is out with Nan in the town at the market, leaving a dish of potted meat in the larder for them to eat when they come home from school, Jill will settle in front of the fire with an apple and Catherine Christian or Ethel Talbot or Bessie Marchant or 'William'. Occasionally a friend will accompany her home, sometimes a girl who lives 'Under the Bridge', on the other side of the tracks – Mildred, or Edith, or Jessie, or Doreen who think Jill lives in a palace because her house has a garden and carpets. Jill has long ago stopped playing Doctors and Nurses or even helping to bath the Avenue baby. Her pleasures are more ambitious, more likely to involve the failure of complicated apparatus such as trying to make a kaleidoscope. But as the nights grow colder, and dark descends before the end of school such ideas are impossible. For a short time that autumn she has written to the girl whose garden abuts on hers, a garden with a 'paddock'. Each day they have written a letter and dropped it in a post-box made from a shoe box nailed to the fence behind the crab-apple tree. Vivian has written long descriptions of her bedroom and clothes and dogs and it has been exciting to find an envelope waiting and to reply. But Vivian has now gone off to boarding school and Jill has never even been invited to tea.

The family only go out to tea at the weekends; visits which Jill enjoys only if she can find books and magazines at the house of the hostess. She has got through a whole year's issue of the *Woman's Journal* in this way. But her parents' friends do not have very interesting books. Her taste is catholic – the *Girls' Crystal* stories eventually mix with the autobiography of a famous feminist, but this winter that pleasure is still a few months away. She is still in Mr George's class and he teases her and calls her a bookworm.

Jill is still a chatterbox and – in spite of the Dream Queens – she likes the company of men.

The war is getting nearer home now and Mr George has received his call-up papers. Jill is more concerned with school feuds and adventures than with the war. It is this autumn that she has stuffed rosehips down the back of Mary's cousin. Rosehips make you terribly itchy and she cannot abide Maggie Ackroyd. The only result though is a deep guilty fear that Maggie's Dad will get her and the police will soon be calling. This happens one evening when there is a ritual hair-washing to be endured at the kitchen sink. Mother has heard that nits are going the rounds and although Jill and Nancy have none, has insisted on dragging a fine comb through their agonised hair. What with this and the fear of Mr Ackroyd's sudden appearance, it is a miserable evening.

*

It was not that Arthur was a nasty boy. Far from it. Although he is the son of a poor farmer and not too clean, Arthur is rather a quiet sort. But he has adenoids, pale blue eyes, a long nose and unkempt hair, and generally gives a 'gormless' impression. He wears a smelly old jacket, stiff old-fashioned boots and stained grey trousers. Jill has the impression that the teachers despise him, but try not to show it.

Her involvement with Arthur all starts as the result of a handwork lesson.

While the girls are doing needlework the boys can make things. Jill never thinks of needlework as making anything; indeed as she never finishes anything, this is the case. She has never finished the first sewing bag started in Standard One in which to put the finished objects.

One afternoon Mr George has set the boys to learn how to back their exercise books. Some unwanted ends of wallpaper rolls have arrived for this purpose from the local paper-hanger. Evidently the boys have been enjoyably busy, tidying up their inky exercise books with the careful pastel shaded zigzags everybody buys for walls. At the end of the lesson, as the girls cluster back to home base the boys are tidying up their scraps. Mr George has been working on their better natures, for it appears that next week the boys are to back the girls' books. Arthur Lewis approaches Jill, his pale eyes shining. 'Can a back yer books next week?' he requests. Jill is torn between feeling flattered that anyone should wish to do her a service and contempt and revulsion for the down-at-heel Arthur who will obviously make a muck of it. But she graciously assents, though she is puzzled why he has chosen her.

In due time Arthur bears her books off to Handwork and returns them at the end of the lesson in not too disreputable a condition. 'Thank you, Arthur,' she says brightly. 'It's very kind of you.' He hangs his head and blushes.

Nothing much happens for a week or two.

It is perhaps unfortunate that one of the local farmers calls for the pig bin which stands in the middle of the Avenue for everyone to fill with potato peelings and other scraps. The farmer is Mr Lewis and Arthur Lewis accompanies him. She is standing at the window when she sees him at the same time as he sees her and he stops open-mouthed with a stupid look on his long face. Jill dives behind the chair, for her hair is wet. Arthur slowly comes round the back of the house where he can be heard gruffly at the back door checking to see if Mother has any more rubbish for his father's pigs.

'He is an *awful* boy,' she says over tea. But why is she so furious? He has backed her books for her, hasn't he?

This is October, the back-end of the year as they call it.

By November Arthur has taken to ringing the bell on his rounds to see if she will come to speak to him. He seems desperate. One November evening when it is already dark and the family is sitting down to sardines on toast, Jill hears the van and the clatter when the bin is emptied. Then, as usual, after a few minutes, the bell.

'Do go and see what he wants.'

'No – you go. I think he's silly.'

Mother goes off and returns to say Arthur wishes for a word with Jill: 'It's important, he said.'

Jill makes her way reluctantly into the kitchen.

Arthur is standing humbly, one large red hand at his side, the other clutching a brown paper bag.

'I've brought you some duck-eggs,' he says, looking up at her as she stands there. 'You'll like them.' There is a great shortage of fresh eggs at this time.

Jill peers inside the bag. Two very large greenish eggs! What should she do? She doesn't fancy anything that comes from that boy's farm. But it is kind of him, she supposes, some sort of tribute.

'Well, thank you. I'll tell my mother. How much?'

'Nay, there's nowt to pay. It's a present,' says Arthur.

Oh, how she wishes he would *go*! The best thing to do to get him on his way is to accept his eggs.

'Mumm-y! Arthur's brought you some eggs!' she bawls.

'They're for *you*,' mutters Arthur.

'Well, thanks again. It's very kind of you.'

Arthur shuffles from one foot to the other.

'And thanks for backing my books,' she adds, then 'Ta-ra,' cheerily, shutting the door with her foot, holding the eggs. Then he *has* to go.

Mother is quite impressed. What a kind boy! They do say the farm is in difficulties, up Holmgate. Arthur's eldest brother has been called up. Arthur spends most of his time helping his father.

'It's in exchange for all our potato peelings, I expect,' says Jill. She wants to pass it off. It is *stupid*. He has embarrassed her in front of her parents. Nancy is gleeful.

'Who's Arthur Lewis's sweetheart?' she chants till Jill fights her and kicks her shins.

If it were only a *presentable* boy, like Dennis Haythornthwaite whose father teaches English at the Grammar School!

She does not try to imagine what Arthur feels, or to imagine that perhaps Arthur's feelings might be compared to some degree with her own for the Dream Queens. That would be ridiculous, for how could anyone feel like that about *her*! What about the tribute of duck eggs then? She cannot eat the great things. Dad makes an omelette of them and says he's often eaten duck eggs on the family farm in the North Riding before the Great War. Arthur does not even ask whether she has enjoyed them so she is spared a fib.

Nothing more happens till Christmas week, except that Arthur swaps desks to be nearer her. She pretends she has not seen him. He does not exactly frighten her, rather repels her – and also annoys her. How can such an awful boy *presume*? Her feelings are not, she thinks, unkind, just bored, incredulous and a little angry.

Things change on December 18th . Jill has celebrated her tenth birthday a week or two before, but Arthur has thankfully not discovered her date of birth, or she shudders to think what further outrage he might perpetrate. However, there is now only a week to Christmas and the school is breaking up on the twentieth. A light powdering of snow has fallen, not enough to sledge on, but enough to build a small snowman.

The first day of the holidays the postman arrives as usual with his bundle of cards. All with red stamps and addressed to Mother and Father to be added to the first arrivals on the sideboard. Things are beginning to feel Christmassy. She rushes to the letter-box and sees an envelope addressed to herself in pencil with a green stamp. For a moment she allows herself to speculate. But she knows, oh, she knows. And it is. Arthur has sent an old card crossed out carefully, a card with purple violets, most un-Christmassy – and 'Love from you know who', again in pencil. Rage fills her. Why *should* she 'know who'? Why cannot it be someone else, some Prince Charming or perhaps Leslie or Mr George – or even Vivian. But she recognises the tell-tale handwriting – debased copperplate as taught at school. How *dare* he presume she will wish to receive one of his grubby offerings? It is worse than the duck egg. She hides it.

But next morning the postman arrives again, this time bearing only one envelope. Miss J Brook, spelt wrongly as usual and a stamp all higgledy-piggledy. And inside a card with imitation lace and this time kisses after a soppy verse. Well, she will just pretend she hasn't got them if she sees him. He hasn't signed his name. It could be anyone!

Unfortunately, Mother pounces on it as it is the postman's only tribute that day. Jill pretends she has no idea who has sent it.

But it does not stop. On Christmas Eve the pig bins are emptied before the feast. Such a clattering and shouting with all the neighbours rushing out with bits of Brussels sprouts and potato peel saved from the pre-Christmas day preparations.

And, of course, there is Arthur in a new pair of wellingtons and a Balaclava helmet. 'Oh, bother him,' she shouts to the window. Is he about to offer the family a turkey perhaps? She laughs grimly – Noël the private detective often does this and she has practised in front of the dressing-table mirror.

The gate clicks open and from behind the curtain she sees Arthur stagger past the snowman bearing something mauve in his hand. The letter-box clicks. He walks away; does not look back; has an attitude of quiet desperation. Three envelopes, one pink, one mauve, one yellow, all with a pencilled name and all, as she realises as she opens them one after the other, all old cards with the names rubbed out and Arthur's hieroglyphics as replacement.

One says: 'From A. Lewis'.

The next says 'With love from Arthur X X X'.

The third says (after a verse of good cheer and the picture of a festal board) – 'Happy Xmas and a Good New Year from yours faithfully Arthur Lewis and Good Luck'.

Five cards in all! Five *old* cards. Five times he has repeated himself. Does he imagine she cannot read? It is pathetic – by multiplying his cards he thinks he can multiply the effect, and that she will be more likely to take notice of him, she supposes. Well, she will just show him.

But she is secretly amazed that such a dull boy – he is dull, there is absolutely no doubt about it, and has nothing to say for himself – that he should bother to find five old Xmas cards, alter them and post them – and even bring them round himself. Fancy even remembering – with all he has to do for his father! She is sorry for him in a way. What does he expect to gain from all this? And although he is not a noisy, aggressive boy, why does he imagine that just because he likes her she will like him? She has a tiny fear about what he will be capable of in the future if he is so bold at eleven. It is unusual. Boys don't usually bother. Perhaps it is because he has older sisters and brothers or because he lives on a farm? Perhaps he is in some curious way grown up?

Whatever the reason, she still considers him a nuisance and gets her revenge in January. Yet when she thinks about it afterwards she is filled with horror at her cruelty.

What happens is quite simple. There has been a fight at the sledging field. Someone has thrown stones; someone else has knocked someone off his sledge.

Jill has seen Arthur and one or two of his friends earlier on in the afternoon. The friends are shouting and waving their arms. She has definitely seen Arthur there. When later there is a fracas and somebody gets his head cut, it is quite likely that Arthur's friends, or even Arthur, has done it, or knows about it, she tells herself.

So that, when Mr Humphrey asks straight after prayers on Monday morning if anyone knows anything about Saturday's incidents – which have been reported to him and are a disgrace to the school – Jill decides – or rather something in her decides – to speak. Her head is pumping with fright and self-importance, but she stands up, as requested, the old tell-tale Jill to the fore, stands up and renounces her swain. Yes, quite a few boys she knows were in the park on Saturday. Well – Trevor Smith for one and Henry Fieldhouse – and er, Arthur Lewis. No, she has not exactly seen them throw stones, but knowing what sort of boys they are, etc. She hears herself breathing, nervous but determined to get her own back. She betrays Arthur Lewis with all the force at her command. The headmaster encourages this sort of thing.

Afterwards, she feels hot and cold, full of shame. But she holds her head high and never once looks at Arthur. That guilty fear of authority she will turn back on someone else. On to poor, unsuspecting Arthur who has probably been innocently sledging all Saturday. She will get her own back, make him hate her, just to earn a pat on the back from Mr Humphrey. She has denounced Arthur in order to suck up to the powerful. Arthur is a born victim. But she does not like herself.

Jill knows she has not been truthful, and very unkind. Arthur teaches her to examine her own motives and not to be seduced ever again into the limelight of finger-pointing and accusation, so miserable is she about herself afterwards, tormented by a bad conscience.

Arthur's father's farm fails soon after and somebody else comes to collect the pig bin's contents.

Jill lets the purple cards lie at the bottom of her handkerchief drawer for a few months until they are replaced by a turquoise pencil, given to her by a tall, smarmy boy whose finger-nails are cleaner than Arthur's.

FIFTEEN

The Facts of Life

The teacher for her last two terms at the village school is her own Aunt May: forty children in her class is a difficult assignment. Jill and her best friends withdraw and write their scrapbooks, or read at the back. Where is Jill to go with her enthusiasms but towards more reading and more writing? She is interested in Jane Austen and Charlotte Brontë, clearly two completely different sorts of women, and therefore completely different kinds of writer. Jill favours the local heroine, Charlotte.

Most of her favourite writers will continue to be women.

When she leaves the Elementary School in the village at the age of ten the headmaster, whom she does not like, surprises Jill by writing in her autograph album:

To thine own self be true
And it must follow as night the day
Thou canst not then be false to any man.

She had not expected such a man to quote from Shakespeare.

*

'Ask Marie,' says Angela.

'*I* dunno,' says Joan.

'See you this aft,' says Joyce.

'Ta-ra,' says Jill. She likes that word, which her mother says is 'common'.

They have been walking home from the special Lent class, held on Thursdays by the curate. Attendance at this 'class', though it is more of a prayer meeting, enables you to receive a purple stamp to stick on a mauve card, one every week till the card is full on Good Friday, and also allows you to avoid sewing lessons. Jill would sell her soul to the Rev. Rabbits's Devil to avoid needlework and she finds the Lent 'specials' quite interesting, though Rabbits tends to say his prayers in a very silly way: 'Aow Lawd lead uss in the parfs of righteousness'. The canon in charge of the village hopes to produce a good number of communicants as a result of these classes, but he has no particular hopes for Jill as she goes to a Chapel Sunday School.

This is the age of the Best Friend. There has already been Margaret in Standard Three the year before who lives on a farm and who has told Jill that when girls are fourteen their wee-wee turns to blood. She whispers this behind her hand and Jill is a little horrified. It is to be another two years before this knowledge is officially sanctioned, when her mother gets round to asking a favour of the mother of her next Best Friend so that the friend might enlighten Jill about periods. By this time Jill already knows about them but when taxed by her mother on a walk to tell her 'what happens to girls when they are about thirteen or fourteen?' can bring out nothing but 'hair under your arms and big bosoms'. She senses her mother's embarrassment, so pretends not to know,

When they are ten, Jill and the next Best Friend, Joan, spend a good deal of time in the school field after hours – they both live near the school – leaving All Bran and even chocolate in the hollow trunk of an oak tree to placate the 'Tree Spirit'. They have a rigmarole to go through before they leave the offerings, have to bow down and bang their heads three times on the ground. The Tree Spirit is more exciting than the God of the Sunday School.

When they leave the village school Jill will be sent to a co-educational Grammar School, but Joan will attend a girls' school in another town. You have the choice of three Grammar schools, which are all free if you are very poor but cost better-off parents either three, five, or nine guineas a term. Joan's school will give proper enlightened talks about periods, and she will impart much technical information to Jill, though nothing about why anyone would want to go in for all this future bodily activity except to make babies.

But for the moment Angela and Marie are talking about something secret with the boys again, in the playground the very next day after the Lent lesson. This time Jill joins the giggling whispers.

'*She* dun't know, does she, what a man and a woman do to have a baby? Go on, tell her, Terry.'

'Yes, I do,' lies Jill.

Marie and Angela take her aside and they walk up into the field from the playground. Jill feels that everybody is talking about this one thing which she has not known – but when enlightened by Angela and Marie she knows that she has always 'known'. How else could it happen – and why bother making men and women different in their bodies unless there is some reason for it?

'And,' concludes Angela, 'even your mum and dad do it.'

'Even the King and Queen?' asks another little girl who has joined the group.

'Course.'

Marie then whispers – hands slyly round mouth, eyes bulging, that Gladys Gallis has *seen it done* – in a field one Saturday afternoon under a wall – and the girl had her knickers off!

The picture is horrible yet fascinating.

'I don't believe it – any of it,' says Joyce.

'Oh, I expect it's true,' says Jill.

'Ooh, you are *awful*.'

'*I* didn't make it up.'

'I know, let's write to Terry and Frank – we could ask them things – pretend we don't know,' says Marie.

'Why?' asks Jill.

'Something to do – see what they say. Get them to write to us.'

The idea is dropped, but discussed again a few days later after playtime when the 'clever' girls in the corner have nothing to do. They are supposed to be copying out poems as they have done all their fraction sums. Marie begins an idle scribble.

'Go on, write the word,' says Joan.

'Oh, *no* – it's rude!'

'I will then – there!' She does. Marie's rather ornate copperplate splutters in the last 'k'. They all peer at it.

'You could be put in prison for *saying* it,' says Joyce.

'But we've only *written* it!'

'Let's ask Terry if he knows what it means.'

Jill has never once heard the word in her whole life. She knows lots of swear words – hell and damn and blast and bloody and, worst of all, bugger. But this one is much worse. It is, she thinks, regarded as the worst sin, even to know it. She does not really see why the word should be so bad in itself. She can see that people regard the action as ugly. Even so, she feels there is one part of the thing that everyone misses out. What is the connection with men and women falling in love? Something must make them want to do this rather peculiar thing. She resolves to consult the library and Saturday afternoon sees her with first the medical dictionary and then the Concise Oxford.

'Sexual intercourse': it sounds very grand and sober. Why is everyone so funny about it? What is there to be ashamed of? Why can't they talk about it as they talk about God or even how babies are born?

Jill looks up from the library table. She is ten, and angry. Yet of course it is *funny* – funny to be laughed at really – to think of all those solemn grown-up people doing it.

But next day at school she keeps her researches to herself and joins in the titters, though she is ashamed to be doing so. Joan and Marie decide to write the word down and send it to Trevor and Derek, Terry and Frank.

'Do you know what this word means?' the first note begins and under the flap Marie prints neatly *the word*. The note is returned and underneath Trevor Marshall has written: 'Yes. Do you? Want to try?'

At playtime Trevor is next to Jill in line. 'Think you know everything!' he hisses in her ear. Jill returns his stare and boldly says: 'Yes.'

'Then what's 'stiff on the bar'?' he asks. Jill doesn't know but tosses her head and replies: 'You always think you know more than we do. Well, you don't.' Further conversation is impossible as they have to march into the big room for a concert. The headmaster is a great one for keeping their spirits up and organises a sing-song every Wednesday.

The next thing that happens is that the group of girls and the boys at the back of the classroom on the other side begin to send each other rude letters and pictures. There is a sort of frenzy about it and Jill shudders when she wonders how it will end. They get her to contribute however, against her will, ruefully and cravenly. She is the best at writing verse and the notes require verses. Frank has started it with a parody of 'Run rabbit, run' which Jill honestly doesn't understand. But she is able to write her parody of 'Daisy, Daisy' – 'David, David,' for Joyce, who thinks David is wonderful:

David, David, give me your answer do,
I'm half crazy, all for the love of you.
It won't be a stylish wedding
We can't afford any bedding –
But you'd look sweet
Sat on the seat
Of a lavatory made for two'.

The last touch is exquisite and reminds her of the farm holiday.

She writes it out for Joyce to send. It is really quite clever, she thinks. But when she gets home, in bed that night she prays to the God of her first years, not the God of the Chapel, for forgiveness. 'I didn't mean to do it. I didn't want to do it. Please forgive me for doing it. And please, please – don't let Mummy find out.'

Worse, much worse is, however, to come. Interest in the filthy notes has slackened somewhat: there is a limit to imagination, even to Marie's, who decorates paper with little semaphore figures all waggling their enormous 'members'.

But one morning a few days later a girl from Standard Six comes in and says that Mr Humphrey wants to see David, Frank, Trevor and Derek in his room, pronto. The boys look guilty and steal a quick glance at the girls who stare down at their books. They depart in single file and do not return. About half an hour later the same message comes requesting the presence of Jill, Joyce, Joan, Marie and Angela in the HM's study. Jill's heart begins to bump with terror. This is it! How can he have found out?

The girls enter the study one by one at intervals. Jill is second, after Joan. The boys are nowhere to be seen.

Mr Humphrey is very angry and barks at her. 'What do you know about this disgusting letter – signed by you, amongst others?'

Jill does not know which letter he has found so says she doesn't know anything.

'Come here, girl. Are you in the habit of writing this *filth*? Are you not *ashamed* of this disgusting display? What would your *family say*? Confess – you are the ringleader. You have profaned this school and abased yourself to amuse these nasty little boys! *Out* with it! A farrago of disgusting lies ... I wish you to *apologise* before I decide on the punishment...'

Jill wants to say: 'Who found it? Who gave it to you?' but

bursts out instead, indignantly with: 'It's *not* lies. It's in the public library! It's *true*. We were only writing the truth!'

'Oh, you were, were you?' He seems at a loss. 'So you thought you would enlighten your little friends with the results of your reading. This will hang over your head all *your life* – Confess and be ashamed and I will decide whether to tell your *parents*.'

'Oh, please sir, don't tell *them*,' Jill bursts out. 'I don't care what you do to *me*, but please don't tell *them*!

'Confess you wrote – a note like this – before I destroy it before your very eyes.'

'I wrote a poem.'

He seems flabbergasted and barks: 'Send in Joyce Ormerod.'

Joyce Ormerod is already in tears and known to be soppy. Jill mouths at her: 'Say nothing,' knowing that Joyce need not incriminate herself. Her father is a Sunday School Superintendent and it would be terrible for him to discover his daughter is a sinner. Mr Humphrey interrupts the glance however.

'Silence Jill Brook. I know your deceitful ways. *You* have led Joyce Ormerod into this disgusting performance. I know a ringleader when I see one!'

'Joyce had nothing to do with it,' Jill gets out.

Mr Humphrey ignores her this time and thunders for the other girls to enter, which they do, one by one, heads hanging, tears at the ready.

Jill does not cry. She is too angry. She knows there is something wrong about it all. They have been silly – but it has not been about a lie. What she has read in the library *is* true, so why can't they explain about it properly – or stop pretending and blustering?

Mr Humphrey seems to have exhausted his powers of rhetoric – 'Never in the history of this school ... I hope never again to have to face corruption in young and innocent children ...'

Then he pulls himself together and puts on his strictest face. 'The boys involved have been caned. You I cannot cane.

You lot will, as you know, be leaving this school for a Grammar School in the summer. Your punishment will be that you will have to live with yourselves for the rest of your lives. You may go now and tell no one of this episode. Grammar Schools do not want dirty-minded children.'

Jill wants to ask: 'But are you going to tell them?' and is about to frame the question when the Headmaster sees it coming. 'No more of your impertinence, Miss. Out you go! You have disappointed my trust in you. I only hope your new school will not discover the depths of your depravity.'

Jill knows she will not do it again, but she is still more angry than sorrowful.

When they have filed out she cannot help wondering what Mr Humphrey does when they have gone. Does he laugh, or groan or put his head in his hands or smile wickedly or draw his writing paper towards him to begin: 'Dear Mr & Mrs Brook – it has come to my notice...' etc., etc.? Her punishment is to be that she will never know and for three years will carry the secret shame within her, with a festering anger at injustice, a fear that her parents might be told, a fear of anyone who knows she has taken part – and that they might tell others. Nightly prayers do not help much.

It transpires later that Joy Gibbs has been collecting the notes, with the intention of ruining Jill and her friends who have for too long received the favours of the staff. Joy has stayed behind at four o'clock each night to pick up the missives, dropped so carelessly from the desks of the group.

Frank and David and the other boys bear their striped palms stoically and say Humphrey is a sod – but you can't cane *girls*. They are surprisingly magnanimous. Jill knows that the girls are just as much to blame. She is sure that the boys don't feel they have been stigmatised or bear a burden of secret guilt into the rest of their lives, although they, unlike her, think the idea behind the word is 'wrong'.

Such is Jill's introduction to the Facts of Life.

Perhaps Mr Humphrey thinks that if Jill is true to herself she will hate the whole idea of 'sexual intercourse'. But she ceases to have much interest in such things for several years, and continues monotonously to fall in love with beautiful women.

Certainly she is being true to herself at such times.

SIXTEEN

Ten Years Old

Some of the Sunday School friends are also friends during the holidays, or after school in summer, or on long Saturday mornings when children are turned out of the house. The 'clubs' they have established are still going strong. The Silver Pin Society has been disbanded but the Swan Club and the Smugglers' Adventure Gang have followed on its demise.

The Swan Club meets to explore the nearest little valley which they christen Swan Valley. The valley, the little stream, the island, the bushy slope, the path at the top to the viaduct crossing, and towering above it all the viaduct itself, built in 1855, are traversed, mapped and written about. They want to chart the source of its stream; they try to build a hut; they discover a culvert. The Club also intend to hollow out a canoe from a fallen tree-trunk, but the task is beyond their penknives. They produce many pages of coloured maps and discover to their amazement how a little brook is *the same stream* in the distant woods of their walks two or three miles away, as the one under the railway viaduct. Further on it joins a large beck, which itself joins the river Calder. The mystique of exploring is intense – the compass, the knapsack, the penknife, the apple, the notebook, the pencil, the whistle – and the special badge.

The interest in boats has arisen from another library discovery, Arthur Ransome, and fits in with Jill's passion for the Navy, fed by the War as well as '*The Fighting Temeraire*'.

Exploring Swan Valley is not frowned upon by the powers that be, but neither is it particularly encouraged. Scrapbooks of the Royal Navy may be worthwhile, but desires for cutters and schooners and trips to the Outer Hebrides are dismissed as moonshine.

There have been earlier walks, without penknives, walks with Aunt May, leading to discoveries of other little streams and woods, always deserted and quiet and beautiful, sometimes sheltering an old water wheel. Jill is convinced when she reads *The Wind in the Willows* during her first term at the Grammar School that the author is talking about 'her' stream when he writes: 'what seemed at first sight like a little landlocked lake ... and ahead of them the silvery shoulder and foamy tumble of a weir.'

Like Mole she wants to gasp: 'O my! O my! O my!' She recognises a poetry of place, and Grahame's words affect her even more profoundly than the real brook she walks by with Aunt May.

English lessons at the village school were called Composition or Poetry. The Poetry resembles the war songs they sing; the noble sentiments declared on England's behalf are on everyone's lips, and join on to the earlier legends of Will Scarlett and his Leafy Forest Bed, Sunset Breezes wafting over England's Heart For Ever, and the Road through the Woods in Our England that will Always Be a Garden. After all, the school is the *National* School, run by the Church of *England*.

By the time they are ten and in the second term of Standard Five, Jill and her friends know they are to go to different Grammar schools after the summer holidays. Of the forty children in the class, eight, mostly girls, have passed the Scholarship. These girls are often bored during lessons and now look for other things to do than write rude letters to boys. They act in plays and 'pageants;' they write letters in code; they practise deaf and dumb language under the desk;

they read all the schoolgirl books and girls' adventure stories they find in classroom cupboards, stories by people like Christine Chandler and May Wynne.

At the weekend the red telephone kiosk is a good place for pranks. You lift the heavy black receiver, and when the operator – who lives in the Exchange not far away – asks for the number you require, you reply in a deep voice: 'This is Funf speaking,' before crashing down the apparatus and haring away down the lane.

When they have no spare pennies for the public telephone they go home and make their own telephones from Bournvita tins and twine, and string them tautly from their bedroom windows across the Avenue – and are amazed when they work. Arthur Mee and his *Children's Encyclopaedia* are responsible for many failed projects, but the telephone tins are a great success.

The spring following Jill's tenth birthday in the winter, she reads a book borrowed by her mother from the library, entitled *Tomorrow Is a New Day*, by a certain Jennie Lee. It is not a story book, but the autobiography of a woman politician, and it impresses Jill so much that she writes a secret pact with herself:

I will prove by word and deed
That women and girls are just as good
In every way as boys and men
If not better.
Signed: JB, Blood Sister to Jennie Lee.

She pricks her thumb and writes her initials in blood.

Much later, she realises that the book has made her what they call a 'feminist'. Formerly she has not wanted to *be* a boy – now she thinks she might. She puzzles over wanting to prove girls 'are as good', for if they *are* as good, why should she need to be a boy? She is not anti-boy, though many boys are a nuisance, and she is still proud to be asked – very occasionally – to play football with them. The idea that girls are 'weak' is silly. But boys have to go in the army and fight and Jill knows she would not be much good in an army – no better than she was at climbing trees. She has identified strongly with Jo March ever since her first reading of *Little Women*, Jo with her temper and her 'scribbles'. Jill has the temper in any case, does not need to cultivate that, but her own 'scribbling' has already been influenced by her heroine. Even the *Plays in Two Volumes*, written before the war in those blue notebooks, started off with *The Children at Christmas* – a Christmas with no presents, in imitation of Louisa Alcott. Jill has already read *Jane Eyre*, and sympathised with Jane, but been furious with her for refusing to live with Mr Rochester after the discovery of his mad wife. Love, she thinks, is much more important than marriage!

Other ideas lead to a play about Florence Nightingale, and to Jill's *Scrapbook of Women Writers*, compiled at school.

She begins then to want to find out about the countries which no one can now visit, but which friends and neighbours, and even her father, visited after the Great War. Switzerland possesses her imagination: mountains and lakes and shining flowers, not to mention Heidi. She produces another ambitious scrapbook which principally consists of beautiful post-cards of Switzerland and Sweden and France, and of girls dressed like the doll Trudy, from the collection of Miss Williams who lives in the next house, who was once a headmistress, and travelled a good deal. Jill adds foreign stamps and paragraphs copied from library books to the postcards, learns the curious German spelling – *Finstaërrhorn* is her favourite – and peppers Composition with her new knowledge. The scrapbook is called, *Countries, Customs and Costumes* which she thinks gives an elegant touch, though she is a bit short on Customs.

Now she wants to learn French, so Mother buys her a book about Madame Souris with pictures and French words.

'*Madame Souris a une maison. La Maison de Madame Souris est petite*,' she repeats.

It is only when the real refugee girl, not just a boring

evacuee, arrives in the village, that Jill is able to put her knowledge to some use. She is determined to bag the Belgian Monica Hodson for her own – with the aim of learning French.

Monique Marie Hélène Madeleine Gilène Jeanne Hodson is a dark girl who smells of home-made bread and who is for ever dissolving into tears. Papa Hodson is British and has brought the family back to his native town from Brussels. They are Catholics, which is additionally fascinating.

'I'll fight you for her,' states Renee Black, a vulpine girl who lives next door to the chimney sweep. Jill has to endure a pinching, shouting, scrabbling match, with Renee's supporters urging on Renee. This battle is on the Stray after school and Monica looks on terrified. Surprisingly Jill wins, and Renee flounces off. It occurs to no one that both girls could be friends with the bewildered Monica.

Jill has Monica to tea and elicits the long name and a few other words. Monica writes in a flowery hand and asks Jill back to her father's temporarily rented house. There are no carpets and the children only have what they stand up in, until Madame Hodson gets to work on the purchase of jumpers for the northern cold. Shortly afterwards, Monica is dispatched to St Joseph's, and her brothers to St Bede's, but their flavour lingers on, and Jill feels she has lost a link with a wider world. She has so wanted to be Monica's best friend but the barriers of language and religion have been too high to be scaled by any of the English children, however much they put their arms round the miserable grey-jerseyed refugee and offer her pieces of home-made cake.

The Bernese Oberland and Monica fall into place as 'phases'. Evacuees go on arriving at different times from London with strange accents and stranger habits, all part of this activity called The War. One or two of them haunt Jill's imagination – a dark girl from the South; a tall blonde from Ilford...

The short prickling of interest caused by what appears to be the entire population of one of the Channel Islands descending upon their little town has subsided. The children are swarthy and have names like Gallis. But they are less exciting than the soldiers who come up not long afterwards in lorries from Dunkirk to be billeted on families in the village.

The lorries pause outside Holm Garth for people to bring out jugs of water, the soldiers are so thirsty. The village post office is the centre of dispersal and the village PC works overtime fitting in haggard young Scotsmen nearly all called Thomas into the clean, small, village houses.

One comes to stay a few days at Jill's house before going home on leave.

'Please give us another soldier,' Jill begs the constable a few days later, 'Mummy loves having them to stay.'

In the deserted former parkland between Rooks Nest and the railway, there are one or two entrances to the shafts of 'clay mines' that have been blocked up for years. But, Jill thinks, who would want clay? – the soil is full of it. She will discover years later that there were once open cast coal pits dotted around the open spaces near the village.

Jill wants to map these shafts and explore their underground reality. The best one is not deep. It is a brick tunnel, open for several yards, coming above ground at an angle of about fifteen degrees. At its inside end, if you penetrate the short, dark, just-underground passage, is a barred wooden door, behind which Jill thinks she hears the sound of rushing water. It is the site perhaps of hidden treasure, or haunted by ghosts or German spies?

Many forays with torches, matches and penknives have proved unsuccessful so that when she persuades their Tommy Number Two from Glasgow to accompany her and some friends down the gently sloping shaft one Saturday afternoon she is hopeful of a Great Adventure. Surely a soldier will know how to open the door?

Once they arrive, however, Tommy is reluctant and becomes stern.

'It's verra – dangerous,' he says slowly – though how does he know? His Scots caution overrides the expedition.

He does, however, play with the children – he is only eighteen – and loads them with keepsakes of French centime pieces with holes in the middle, souvenirs of Dunkirk.

The Tommies follow each other on leave to Scotland and are never seen again, though both write to thank their hosts for their hospitality.

War has pointed all the children in the direction of adventure, thrills, danger. They invent secret codes, and Jill makes another scrapbook, this time of photographs of warships cut from the daily newspaper. Day by day the scissors crash through the *News Chronicle*, cutting destroyer after destroyer and all anecdotes of the Senior Service. It is regarded as a worthwhile if rather masculine interest as it is clearly to do with the War Effort.

The friends' War Effort now changes gear. Spies haunt all their imaginations. Some think they see a flashing light at the top of the Chapel spire. As the Minister is a Pacifist, some say he is signalling to the Germans in Morse. Jill learns Morse but never sees a flash. But the Smugglers' Adventure Gang do investigate the haunted house, the one next to Brown Owl's, which has been abandoned because it is subsiding into the so-called clay mines that are apparently underneath it. Jill vaguely supposes the mine to be connected with one of the entrances they have unsuccessfully tried to breach, but no one's knowledge goes any further.

The Smugglers' Adventure Gang make the garden of the house their HQ and it is from here that the Spy Plan is conceived. An imaginary spy, Hans Didcot, takes up his HQ there (the cellars have been used by pre-war tramps) and his 'messages' – intended to baffle and frighten her enemies in Standard Five, typed on pink paper on Father's tiny old portable – are a mixture of imaginary 'German' (much swearing of oaths – *Mein Hindenberg – Donner und Blitzen*) and English. These messages are weighted with stones and left in the snicket whose wall abuts the end of the school field, formerly a fold where sheep once grazed. Triumphant friends will arrive at school waving the messages they have 'found,' until eventually one or two of the 'enemies' is persuaded to 'find' a similar one, ready under its stone for playtime. The message speaks mysteriously of waiting till nightfall for the contact to arrive and swearing allegiance to Herr Hitler.

In the end all this misfires terribly. The enemies bear away the message, intending to acquaint the headmaster and the police. Such an irruption of reality into the spy saga is impossible. The enemies are being uncharacteristically pro-authority and have finally to be disabused during a grand battle of Goose Grass, when the Smugglers' Adventure Gang confess they made it all up. The enemy takes quite a bit of persuading and threatens to tell the police anyway that people are *pretending to be spies* – and deserve prison, or worse, for baffling the patriotic.

For weeks, Jill expects a policeman to arrive on her doorstep with a gruff 'Did you write this?'

It is amazing that they have time to learn anything at school, so fully is their time now occupied learning French, exploring, writing plays, reading the *Girls' Crystal*, day-dreaming about 'doubles', cutting poems from the *News Chronicle* now, as well as warships, practising the piano, still rushing twice every Sunday to Sunday School, still collecting stamps, being Brownies, trying to learn Semaphore and Morse – succeeding better with Deaf and Dumb language – sitting examinations for the Grammar School and continuing with the Swan Club, whose new written constitution, closely modelled on the Swallows and Amazons, enjoins its members to continue to make canoes from fallen trees, map streams to their source and build huts in the valley from brushwood.

But the practical explorations by the club will be linked to a twelve chapter, one-hundred-and-fifty-page saga, begun in delirium and ending in dogged boredom, taking place entirely at sea: Jill's first novel, completed at the age of twelve.

After this she will start to write the story of a girl named Joanna who has fair hair and runs out of the house in the early morning to 'dabble in the dew'. The imaginary friends will become Ruth and Carola who progress – in stories – to London, 'after the war,' where they establish a delightful studio in Chelsea. The Family Trees will become *The Broughtons*, begun one Christmas Eve, a long story recorded in old Mill ledgers by Jill's new fountain pen.

The passionate 'phases' will turn into a greedy diving for knowledge in the pool of the unknown and a constant attempt to write about past place and past time. The Hall, The Snow, The Moor, and the old mansion Rooks Nest are also waiting to be 'rediscovered' one day far in the future.

The friends fill their days and summer evenings with other strange activities as they wait to leave the Elementary School. There is still the ritual obeisance – in worship of the Tree Spirit, who now occasionally receives a precious 2*d* Cadbury's bar, the offering always mysteriously gone by morning.

The two friends make enthusiastic plans to go as missionaries – of the Tree Spirit? – to darkest Northern Rhodesia, to a place called Mbereshi, to 'teach the Africans to read'.

Jill also nurtures fantasies of going back in time at Sheepden Hall, for her favourite novel is now Alison Uttley's *A Traveller in Time*. She and Nancy repeat their favourite bit of the story to each other, when Penelope's Aunt Tissie says to the girl – in love with a man who has been dead for nearly four hundred years – '"Of course you will marry, my dear!" But to myself I murmured, "Oh Francis! Francis!"'

In spite of the disappointment of the subject of the Composition required for the Scholarship examination one February morning – 'Suppose you could be someone else. Describe whom you would choose to be' – the attempts must have been literate, since Jill and her three friends are among those selected for the Grammar School. Jill had not been able think of anyone else she would rather be but, assuming she had to think of somebody, opted for the future Queen of England.

There are four Grammar schools close by and one further away in Woolsford. Mother decides that as Jill has no brothers she ought to go to a co-educational one.

Henceforth ‘learning’ will be channelled into ‘subjects’, and Jill will have to wear uniform, and go to school on a bus.
She is thrilled.

SEVENTEEN

Goodbye to Childhood

Jill's mother is No Nonsense and Down-to-Earth, and Jill knows she is a martyr to the housework she dislikes but does so well. She also has a quick temper which she has handed down to her elder daughter, for Jill is impatient, impulsive. She is told she has an exhibitionist streak, and there is nothing worse than showing off, because then you are 'getting above yourself'. On the other hand, once her anger is over, sulks do not follow.

Where Mother is down to earth and quick, Father is slow, and obstinate. He is not unsociable, has friends with whom he sometimes has a pint of beer on a Sunday, enjoys debating and discussing, but does not play golf, as do his father and sister.

One day Jill learns the word 'slump', which Mother talks about more than Father ever does, even though it affects the family business: the mill. Father still endures his work there rather than getting much satisfaction from it. He is more remote than Mother, still does not impinge so much on his children's lives, though gradually the books that have always been part of him become part of Jill, the names of the books an invitation to read them one day: *Bliss*, *The White Peacock*, *Crome Yellow*...

Jill realises one day that her father, like many of his favourite poets, is a Romantic, and that she is too. Once, Father had just as much ambition as she is beginning to find in herself. Ever since she can remember, his poems and plays and short stories have been hidden in cases and tea chests, kept in the box room under dust sheets. Keats is Father's favourite poet, but he also loves the eighteenth century. He wrote verse much influenced by Keats when he was only fifteen and the first book he bought for himself was, he tells her, Johnson's *Lives of the Poets*. He is often found reading George Saintsbury's *Peace of the Augustans*. He is a little sceptical of the vogue for education, which he acquired for himself after leaving a Grammar School. Mother likes poetry too, and during his courtship of her received many poems from Father. She will recite 'Ode to a Nightingale' alone in her bedroom when she is unhappy.

There is a black medallion over Father's bookcase. It is the profile in relief of beautiful Rupert Brooke, a poet, who wrote, 'If I should die, think only this of me'.

Father's first allegiance is to poetry. It is a long time before Jill discovers that this poet was not killed in Flanders, as she has supposed, had nothing to do with the poppies in Flanders Fields, or the roses of Picardy, that people will sing, if given half a chance, at amateur concerts in the park, after the next war arrives. She can recite the first verse of: 'In Flanders Fields':

In Flanders fields the poppies blow
Between the crosses, row on row
That mark our place, and in the sky
The larks, still bravely singing, fly
Scarce heard amid the guns below.

When Jill's father found little success with his writing, which was by the time of his marriage, he continued to read Belles Lettres, and now turns each winter to writing a paper for the Woolsford English Society about one of his favourite writers, usually a relatively unknown one: Norman Douglas, T W H Crosland, William Gerhardie. Jill admires the way he sits down at the table in the dining room on winter evenings, and writes, oblivious to conversation or the wireless, to which Mother listens as she darns the family socks.

Jill sees that her mother would have made a successful man if she had been born a boy. Father is not effeminate but he is not a 'man's man'. There is still a tug of war between the personalities of Jill's two parents, between the 'actress' and the 'writer', that is also a conflict – or at least a difference – between being talkative and concentrating on your inner voice.The same conflict as between playing out and reading.

She and Nancy realise that Mother 'does more for them', as she is always telling them, but they are sorry for their father. He hardly ever gets cross; it is amazing. Much later, when Jill has to choose at school between Art and Latin, and perforce chooses Latin – which Father hasn't studied but Mother has – she will feel it is a choice between the two of them. Mother is much more conventional, or perhaps more aware of social expectations, and did much better at school than her husband, was good at subjects like Algebra and Latin. It is true that Jill has inherited some of her mother's exhibitionism, if none of her singing and sporting prowess, but her enthusiastic temperament appears to come from nowhere, just as her old propensity for being car-sick was not shared by anyone else. 'Not wanting to miss anything' is part of Jill, like her clumsiness, and her physical timidity, so unlike Mother.

Jill's enthusiasms are taken up one after the other, with hardly any breathing space; some of them begin to be connected with a world outside home and school. Hundreds of hours have already been spent reading and writing in Standards Three and Four and Five of the Elementary school, as well as at home. At the Grammar School, Jill will need nobody to tell *her* how important literature is. Later, there will be a conflict between her father's and her own natural Platonism and the Feminism she has discovered for herself, for Father is not a Feminist. He bought all D H Lawrence's novels when he was a young man and Jill and Nancy eventually discover Ursula Brangwen. Jill thinks later that if she had been a boy she might have agreed with Lawrence's ideas. When she is fourteen she calculates she might even have been conceived the very moment D H Lawrence died!

For almost eleven years Jill has lived the life of a child and there have been many pleasures as well as pains ... pleasures arising from colours and smells: the colours of childhood; the dusky pink of mother's best dress with its boxy pleats and padded shoulders; powder blue – her best friend's favourite colour; green and yellow, her own early preference, used for the bands of ribbon in the paintings of Easter Eggs in Standard Two and for the ornamental borders wreathed round the poems they were given to copy. Other colours she disliked, boring ones like beige, though the word was fascinating; fawn, the colour of those long ribbed stockings that always fell around her matchstick legs; 'nigger' brown, colour of her soft velour first school hat: hardly colours at all. Pink-and-blue together were beautiful, and blue-and-yellow found together in fields or pictures. Pink-and-silver was entwined in that bridesmaid posy, yet connected always in her mind with the field of waving, brassy buttercups glimpsed the same day, the whole carpeted sheen of them waving in the Saturday-eleven-o'-clock-in-the-morning-sun... Would Pink be cross if she preferred Yellow, she had wondered in the wedding taxi? Blue-and-silver were the colours of the month of May in a poem read by Miss K, and white was daisies with their faint warm scent when, nose to the lawn, she lay sniffing them at Holm Garth before going into the garden shed that was hot inside and smelled of creosote. She wondered then if *she* had a smell and sniffed the skin on her arm which had a faint aroma, not exactly the smell of soap...

The other Granny's house has another lovely smell. On her chest of drawers in her little back bedroom she has a glass bottle, now empty, that smells faintly of eau de cologne. But if you lean out of the window, the scent of her wallflowers drifts up and Jill wishes she could stopper their scent in the bottle.

In the New House Jill was to be overwhelmed by roses: bright pink single ramblers – Chaplin's Pink; dark pink climbers and others, pale pink, more tightly scrolled, scented ramblers called Cornelia that her father made grow all over the rustic fence and twined in hundreds of scented whorls round the dust-bin. Profuse, almost *too many*. Jill feels an inability to assimilate them, to encompass plenitude. What to do with these feelings of too-much-ness? Certainly not waste the feeling! It will go into compositions or poems. When Jill is eleven, Aunt May is very pleased to receive a poem from her niece on her own forty-eighth birthday:

I Love Life!

For the beauty of the sunrise.
For the splendour of the sunset.
For stirring music.
For the rustling wind.
For the glory of the sun
For murmuring brooks
For moors wild and desolate.
For rich green valleys and graceful trees.
For wonderful poetry.
For marvellous paintings and delicate colours.
For friendship warm and lovely
For loneliness and solitude.
For thoughts and dreams of a better world.
For freedom and security.
For feeling and sympathy.
For rain in storms or showers.
For flowers scented and beautiful.
For warm firesides and homely love.

For the happiness of being outdoors.
For games and the sense of comradeship.
For true love and all that it means.
For peace, sleep, little children, stories.
For brave heroes and patient women.
For life!

By the time she is eleven Jill often thinks about the past. So many people have come and gone...

Long long ago there was Great Grandma who once lived in a house near a big advertisement of a Drummer Boy painted on the end of the terrace. A tiny figure in black, with a shawl and button boots, she was born in 1851 and sat usually by the fire in her special Windsor chair. Her skin was yellowish with cracks in it, and Jill used to hold her breath when she kissed her for she thought she smelled sour. Her hair was white but she must once have been dark-haired. Her legs were too short to reach the ground and dangled in black boots.

She had been well known in the district for her fierceness, and her tailoring and sewing on her old treadle sewing machine, without even a pattern to go by. After her husband died she sewed shirts till the youngest of her nine children was earning, and she outlived her husband by forty-three years. She kept her Norfolk accent, but her daughter, Mother's mother, Granny Wood, 'talks Yorkshire'. Something a bit like the Norfolk accent returns with the evacuees.

Granny Wood is as hard-working as her own mother, but still manages to find time to read three library books each week. She loves a gossip and Jill listens in fascination to the 'Then she sez ... and I sezes.' She is full of herbal lore and can make a meal from a few kidneys, a few carrots and an onion. She is much poorer than the other Granny, and very proud. She has two half sisters and two full sisters as well as three brothers. Her father, once a coachman for a Norfolk landowner, had moved with his second wife to the north for work. It was said by Granny that he read the Dickens serials aloud to work-mates every week, for they were illiterate. Granny keeps up a correspondence with her husband's third cousins in Ontario, Canada. She likes writing.

Good with her hands, like her own mother and her granddaughter Nancy, Granny Wood sews and knits and 'makes do'. Out of all her many children it was with her that Great Grandma went to live when she was eighty. She spent the day mostly in the warm kitchen, though there was a sitting room with a green moquette sofa and chairs, and a cupboard with many interesting things: a heavy photograph album with pictures of more relations, long dead, and Granny's niece's thick school-story annuals from the twenties.

All Granny's family are musical; she has a low contralto and perfect pitch. She was a strong Methodist, met her husband in the Methodist choir where he sang tenor. She shops in the market every day, and daily scrubs her doorstep clean before whitening it with a donkey stone. She has a dry wit and looks at life unblinkingly, disapproving of the immoral capers of some of her relatives. Her half sister married well and is at one time the mayoress of the town. They remained close, for that sister had not said No to making toffee in a back kitchen before her husband's firm took off and became quite famous. But Granny Wood cannot stand another of her sisters, red-haired and 'actressy' as she is. Great Grandma's own sister too had 'run away to go on the stage'.

Jill's two grandmothers have very different ways of carrying on.

Father's mother is placid, rather stately, taller than the other women in the family, blonde and blue-eyed, full-bosomed, Roman-nosed, a woman who likes the pretty things of life and is an excellent housekeeper. Mother hints she is not much of a reader, though Jill knows she reads the *Sunday Chronicle* because once there was a story about an 'immortal' child in it, which Granny half-believed. She is a truly kind woman. Once in Woolsford she is shopping with Jill in Woolworth's and there is a little dirty barefoot boy. She buys him a pair of plimsolls saying: 'I don't like to see that.' She has hundreds of cousins in Nottinghamshire and Lincolnshire; several are always coming to stay at Holm Garth.

Granny adored her husband. When he dies she is bereft, sits in her chair by the window with a balled-up lace handkerchief in the palm of her hand, her eyes full of tears. But when Jill comes into the room she tries to rouse herself, asking her usual question: 'Anything fresh?' She talks about not sending things to the laundry: 'How would you know whose dirty things were near your own?' Her friend and rival Mrs Robinson agrees, so they both wash everything at home in a copper.

Granny talks about the 'nights drawing in'. She and Auntie May sit in the dusk, and then the dark, never putting on the lights till it is really dark.

They sit, not talking much, just thinking – very peaceful. Granny often just watches the gate to see what is happening, though you can't see very much. When Jill arrives for her music lesson every Thursday and the three of them have tea afterwards, Granny always asks for news and gossip.

'Anything fresh?'

Oh, so many people have come and gone: the strange Mrs N-B who drinks, and is often drunk, and lies, face red and hair grey, like a brown paper parcel in the middle of the road, still wearing her green hat and her fawn belted coat. She is a very rich woman, so the policeman is always polite and sends someone to collect her. There is the very strange woman in the long mac and beret who mutters and stares at you with poached-egg eyes; there is the brown skinned baby who is always dressed in yellow – so pretty, both Jill and Nancy think.

There is the big girl who did not approve of the presents Mother had bought for the children to take away after Jill's party, presents of crystal necklaces. She sneered, 'What a strange thing to give us!' Jill was angry. Mother had gone to such trouble.

There are all the children who have gone away. A large pale girl called Wanda, with thick glasses and a scar from a hare lip, poor Wanda, a refugee, whom Jill teaches English words like ladybirds and sticklebacks. 'Don't forget, Wanda,' Jill says. Wanda will not forget. And Velma, a girl with such a curious name that Jill asks her where it comes from and Velma replies: 'It was the chocolate my Dad liked so he called me after it.'

Objects have been used and forgotten, like the sputtering steel nibs at the Elementary School, dipped into inkwells that fit into a hole in the narrow desk, whose depths concealed dampened whorls of dust, dyed dark blue, hanging like seaweed trawled up from the depths. The worst boy in the class who had sat next to her in Standard Three had spattered that ink on purpose all over her work – a big, irregular navy blue splodge disfiguring the whole page. She had 'told of' him to Miss Askrigg who had sorrowfully said she was aware of the problem.

'I'll bash you at home time,' that boy had said. Some National School boys never stopped talking about bashing and 'braying'.

But now Jill will leave the village school where the Three Rs have been drilled into the short-back-and-sides of the boys and the ringleted girls with monotonous precision, where multiplication and the catechism have been learned 'by heart', and where girls have usually been keener to learn than boys who have spent a good deal of time fighting.

At playtime they have played Keys or Statues and raced each other down the long school field. Jill has never been any good at skipping or patting balls in intricate patterns under and over arms and legs, against walls, or doing handstands. Some girls can even walk on their hands but all Jill can manage is a somersault. At first she has fallen down a good deal, scraping her knees. Several older girls have attempted to mother her, which has annoyed her. Other girls have been very fierce and there have been fights.

The girls have been the ones to know all the games and

the rhymes, the ones who can skip so well, even jumping rhythmically over the long rope they borrow every playtime, chanting

Nebuchadnezzar King of the Jews
Bought his wife a pair of shoes
When the shoes began to wear,
Nebuchadnezzar began to swear,
When the swearing began to stop,
Nebuchadnezzar bought a shop
When the shop began to sell,
Nebuchadnezzar bought a bell,
When the bell began to ring,
Nebuchadnezzar began to sing...

Jill has learned her copperplate, staying in at playtime to master the half downward and then half upward stroke of the 'b' which joins it to the next letter. She has learned the difference between 'its' and 'it's', has attended lessons of Drill and Nature Study, Religious Instruction, Drawing, Painting and Poetry, Arithmetic (long division, multiplication and division of fractions both vulgar and decimal), Needlework, Composition, Reading Aloud and Mental Arithmetic.

All have been offered and mostly enjoyed by Jill through the five Standards she has gone through by the age of ten, before the Scholarship is to take her away for ever from that school, built originally for the 'Education of the Poor in the Principles of the Established Church'. Now that she is to go to the Grammar School, she will have to get up when it is still dark and wear the 'bottle green' uniform, to which she is at first very attached.

But she will not forget the children left behind for ever. Her close friends – her first best friend, Joyce, of course, and Jean and Joan, and Dorothy, with the cow-like brown eyes, and Marian and her brother Harold, Edith and her brother Donald, Harold and George, the Canadian twins who wore leather balaclava helmets, and Nan, who moved away when

Jill was seven but was a best friend for six months ... Roy and his cousin Tony; and Brian; and Gladys, Mona, Ruth and Daniel from the Channel Islands. And John and his brother Martin whom she looked after when he was a baby and helped to bathe in her maternity nurse phase when she made notes about First Aid and wheeled Martin in his pram up and down the Drive.

There were two Margarets, and two Davids and a Frank; and Arthur Lewis and his sister Doreen, and Constance, and Pat and Dennis and the John-who-gave-her-the-turquoise-pencil, and Milton and Walter and Christopher and Rachel and Terry and Yvonne and Michael and Virginia and Myra and Alma and Peggy and Joy and Jacqueline and Harry and another Arthur; Betty and Stella and Peter and another Betty, and Pat and Susan and George and another David, and Richard and Ann and Mary and Janet and Cliff. There were the 'poor' girls, Mildred and Doreen. Some of the bolder poor girls could be frightening, but it was a good idea to be on their side in case their brothers were nasty to you. She had liked some of the poor girls – they were kind and wanted to put their arms around you if you fell and grazed your knee: Little Mothers. One or two of them though could be nasty and liked fighting but Jill had sometimes challenged them to fight first.

There was Angela Rose and Sheila, and there were Geoffrey and Andrew, and two more Marys, and Velma-whose-father-named-her-after-the-chocolate and Monique and François and Jean, the Belgians, and Marion, and the twins Nancy and Jenny who did the best handstands...

The war has been only as important as changing schools or moving house, less important than Grandpa's death. Jill continues to love those at Holm Garth who continue to mourn inconsolably, wearing black dresses and coats, which they modify, after a year, to grey and then, after another year, to mauve. It is considered 'common' to wear a black armband. Children are not expected to wear mourning colours, but

Jill's aversion to grey probably dates from this time. After the war the custom goes into decline – the war hurried it on when coupons were needed for new clothes.

The grandparents are connected both to a past Jill has known and one she has not experienced: a family past that comes alive on the Family Trees her aunt continues to elaborate for her, and in that heavy gold-framed portrait of Great Great Grandfather that still hangs in the hall of Holm Garth.

Jill becomes nostalgic for her own past. She finds the negatives of some photographs taken by Aunt May about four years earlier, an age ago, a vanished age: Before the War. During one of her enthusiasms she redevelops them, the procedure involving a small tin bath of hypo and some printing paper bought at the chemists, and a further perusal of the bound volumes of the *Children's Encyclopaedia.* This time the instructions work better than those for making a kaleidoscope, which defeated her. Like the telephones it is to be another success! She sniffs the odour of the crystals with pleasure and watches as tiny photographs reappear slowly, 'as if by magic'.

Holidays ... the hotel in Bridlington where they ate in a private dining room because Granny and Grandpa and Aunt May were staying there too; the long stretches of ridged sand with the wet squiggles left by sand-worms; the tiny snails sticking to the railings on the way down to the beach, and that smell of the sea that was almost better than any other smell ... The harbour with the boat called the *Royal Sovereign* that took people out to sea, with Flamborough Head and the cliffs always there in the distance ... She still has a model of that boat, with sails, but there is nowhere to sail it. The brooks near home are too rapidly rushing or too shallow.

... The holiday in Wharfedale when the hated Pig surprised her; the holiday in Gloucester with Uncle Ned who had a share in a biplane and who called her Rabbit Pie, and where there was – Jill was sure – Mr Macgregor's market garden. They went to the pictures in Gloucester and she saw a film with a thunderstorm and a man called Robert Taylor who was very handsome. No more holidays now because of the war, except close by on a Heptonstall farm. No more holidays on the east coast for five years, and they do not even go to the coast of Lancashire – which is not so nice – for another three. Holidays are exceptional and will always be remembered. But how safe life seems to be, even though they are in the middle of a war. Nobody seems afraid.

Weekly activities will occur predictably, for years. Homework, and music lessons with their attendant examinations, and reading and walks and outings to places further away. To York, the first time she is old enough to realise that the buildings she sees are not black with industry-corrupted millstone grit, and glimpses a countryside which is not hilly.

But one evening, alone in the school field at dusk, just before she starts at the new school, Jill has the sudden realisation of an idea which she has not tried before to put into words.

It comes to her as two words: Reason and Feeling. She thinks, what is called Reason is opposed to what is called Feeling. Is it because of that scrapbook of women writers? Is it because she has conceived the idea that Jane Austen, whom she has not yet read, and Charlotte Brontë, whom she has, stand for these opposed ideas?

Whatever the background to this sudden flash of insight, she knows without doubt that she belongs to the Feeling side. If she ever has to choose between these ways of looking at the world, these ways of Being, she will be compelled to choose Feeling. She will be incapable of choosing Reason. Even so, she tries to reason out this feeling of choice and inevitability. It is true there is never a Reason for her adoration of the Dream Queens. Reason has nothing to do with love. She is aware that others may think her wrong to choose as she does, but this only makes her even more determined to go on feeling, even if the opposition may be partially imaginary. People have called her sorts of feelings 'sentimental'. It is another word she likes, though she has been puzzled by its link with the word 'sensibility', and wonders why one word is 'good' and the other 'bad'.

After the month-long summer holiday, which is always in August, she goes off to the Grammar School on the tenth of September. No longer matchsticks or Brainbox, no longer afraid of pigs, with less time to gather wild flowers.

She will continue to read whenever she can, will write her own stories at home in private notebooks just as she has always done. Sometimes she will describe her private feelings in her new English essay homework now that Composition is to be called 'English'. She will write of snow and winter sunsets, the town band playing 'Christians Awake', the Yorkshire carol, on a Christmas morning, and of her favourite place, Rooks Nest...

Imagination may instigate new fears, as it may work upon perfectly real ones. Imagination will work too upon love of place and make a paradise or a magic realm from an ordinary locale. It has not been necessary for her to imagine Swan Valley; the place was real enough and will become the starting-point for many a daydream, and some nightmares.

Little Boy Blue returns sometimes as the embodiment of summer, as real as hay or porridge, for when she takes the walk down to the Holm Farm, she knows that he still belongs there, and when they make hay by the deserted lake at Rooks Nest, Boy Blue is watching. Even when she is almost grown up walking down the old Coach Road on summer afternoons, or further north as far as the woods near Norwood, Jill feels Boy Blue's presence among the white carpets of daisies that smell slightly of wind and grass and whiteness. Or he may be bathing his feet in the kingcup brook.

Words will link the 'real' real with the imaginary real. The blue and silver in the poem they were taught on May Day by Miss K has 'become' May, and the word for the month still means all that month was, and more. The memory of the bitter gold scent of chrysanthemums is fixed by the name of the flower, that bears the meaning of massed petals in green vases at the Harvest Festival.

Jill is still not sure whether she feels most the real flower or the real scent or the real month or the words given to them or written about them. As time goes on the words may be read detachedly and become something she has never seen, which arouses more powerful feelings than anything she has. Is it somehow cheating to feel like this? If the words are used for thinking complicated thoughts, she feels easier. She is even a little ashamed at being moved by memories and words. Dreaming is not a good thing to do, they say, unless you are in bed. Perhaps that is why she once felt on Little Boy Blue's side in this matter. Later still she puts it to herself that the words *are* her feelings, and writes clumsy verse and word pictures to try and pin those feelings down. She knows they are not good poems but they are pure expressions of feeling. Sometimes though, she hugs the feelings to herself, does not wish to share them with others, or even to admit that the feelings of other people on hearing a poem or a piece of music can be like her own. When her childhood is beginning to end she is glad to find that they can, and eager also to make others feel the same. It is very hard to pin down the feelings. When she believes she has done so and writes an especially good composition at the Grammar school, it comes back with a less good mark and 'try to write more tidily' scrawled over it. She has tried to capture for the English master a sunrise at the beginning of a hot June day with the smell of the early morning garden, blue and purple lupins with their subtle scent, rambler roses – cream, pale pink and dark pink, tumbling out into the dawn towards the sun. She has caught at words to express this beauty and the excitement later in the morning of walking in the green woods with the sound of the beck never far away. But she can never do it satisfactorily, and this piece is 'not up to your usual standard'. The strength of her feelings is evinced in helter-skelter handwriting, over-riding any attempts at neatness, and the feelings themselves have begun to evanesce as she tries to capture them. Yet she knows that it is a sincere attempt, even if it has failed, and is better than her 'Conversation between a Cloud and the Sea', the term before, which came completely out of her head.

Each first feeling is magical, its repetition only echoing the earlier magic. Sometimes it is all too much; the only thing to do is write about it. Soon these feelings will involve walks on the moors, early sunsets, and carols round the Grammar School Christmas Tree. She makes long catalogues of her enthusiasms.

Aunt May remains sympathetic to Jill when adolescence begins to throw its subjective veil between emotions and their objects. The original gulf Jill has clearly glimpsed between Reason and Feeling arrived unbidden; later it will begin to seem applicable to many departments of life and she will not question it for years. It joins the abstractions that will become part of her adolescence, her father's:

Beauty is Truth, Truth Beauty
That is all ye know on earth and all ye need to know...

Beauty is easier to understand than Truth. It takes time to realise that Truth does not mean the opposite of telling lies, but is connected with the reality of both Feeling and Reason. The dreams and the feelings become the Real, and 'real' life merges only partially with the self that feels and dreams. The inner self emerges and thrusts itself against the outer, no longer accepting it. Sometimes the outer goes on fuelling the inner as happens with the places she loves, above all Rooks Nest, the half-ruined eighteenth-century mansion in its park by the elm trees. She will struggle to make art from it but it seems better suited to fantasy.

Rooks Nest has a deserted lake choked with weeds surrounding a laurel-planted island. On the lake shore there is a half sunken skiff, once, Jill imagines, piled high with dark red cushions. Rooks Nest, with its still-standing summerhouse, its long sandy drive and abandoned stables, its tinkling smashed hothouses and rain-pocked statues, its dogs' graves, will feed a stream of invention and half recollection, half history, half fiction, and will lodge itself as a myth in some almost conscious part of her mind.

No book or sentimental poem is responsible for her feelings about this house, built more than a hundred and fifty years before she was born, less than a mile away from her birthplace. It has been waiting for her, quite undramatically, and she incorporates it into her imagined life. It stands, separate from her reading, separate from her loves, linked to childhood and to a possible future of invention. Reason tries to dislodge it later with talk of contingency – 'It could have been any old house' – but racial memory is too deep cut and is planted in a fertile field.

Ten, eleven, twelve, thirteen, fourteen: a lifetime of school. Jill finds many new friends, enjoys everything except drawing birds' bones, needlework, cookery and the wall-bars in the gymnasium. Busy years, happy wartime years in a well-run, settled small community. Some children's fathers are manual workers who want them to get on. Other fathers send off their daughters to boarding school at twelve.

There are school societies, a school magazine, a choir, a sports day, a house system, a uniform, an assembly every morning in the oak-panelled hall, and a speech day at which Jill receives yearly prizes.

In her first year there is also Miss Dunfermline who has dark curly hair and teaches French, or rather 'phonetics', so that they will all end up with a good French accent. But she leaves to get married. Jill gives her a glass napkin ring, begged from home.

Miss Dunfermline writes in Jill's autograph book, and so does her fiancé who comes to the school on a visit. Jill has already made up stories which have included herself as a sort of maid or companion to the pretty young woman, but when Miss D leaves it will be to go to the husband, Robbie. It is difficult to fit him into the daydream, and Miss D loves her swain. In the end Jill sends herself on imaginary visits to the woman, whenever Robbie is abroad.

About two years later, they hear that the real Robbie has been killed in a car smash on the Gold Coast, where he was on some official war work.

Jill remembers Brown Owl's death.

Did she choose these women because their lives were to be tragic?

Two years later when she is almost fourteen she falls in love again and will remain in love for three long years.

But that is another story.

EIGHTEEN

Spots of Time

Jill is seventeen. Memories of her early childhood and of her seven Grammar School years stay with her: the drone of distant cars as she crouched sniffing the catmint in the garden; the jewelled rings in the miniature crackers the second Christmas of the war; the orange and yellow and white flowered cotton dress with its wide sleeve bands, the turquoise velvet dress with its lace collar; the new school uniform so proudly worn; the dappled walks in nearby woods when the stream was the stream in *The Wind in the Willows*; the first sight of the Langdale Pikes on her first visit to Westmoreland in the middle of the war. That had been on a hot summer's day with the scent of pines in the fern-banked woods that sloped down to Windermere. Entering York Minster for the first time; the moon seen through scudding clouds from the bedroom window as she wrote a poem; walking on the nearer moors with friends, and the rare moments of solitude there when the others were ahead or behind and there was nothing visible but loneliness; the motes in the bands of sunlight on the top corridor at school one day when everything was hushed and mysterious, yet clear...

Snow in Oxford, on The Broad, on her first visit there for

interview when she bought a little green leather-bound *Tonio Kröger* at Blackwells; all the magical beginnings of stories, especially the one begun by the gas fire at the end of a Christmas Day; and her imaginary girls: Joanna in the dewy grass, and Ruth, and Margot, invented in the winter firelight.

Jill puzzles over how to describe the involuntary memories that come in the train of that most powerful of all senses, smell, that always brings back the past most powerfully: the natural scents – the grass and snow of long past years, and the smell of the bread Aunt Jenny baked every Thursday in the First House, and put down in the hearth in a big bowl to rise. There was the dark ruby-red smell of the Anglican church, incense lingering from the forbidden practices of the Anglo-Catholic vicar; the sour smell of little boys' clothes that were rarely cleaned; the crisp smell of cotton dresses freshly washed, drying in the sun between two props in the back garden; and the slimy smell of the flower water in the cemetery outhouse that was no less pleasant, taking her back to the cemetery and the peaceful walks, with Nancy in the push-chair.

There was Joan's smell, of cinnamon and gingerbread from her Aga-warmed kitchen, a delicious homely fragrance that permeated Joan's jersey; the smell of picric lint in the dolls' First Aid box, of Germolene, of aniseed balls, of nail varnish, of the new Quink ink; the clean honey-smell of the soap Easter eggs Granny Brook gave them when she was seven. And Father's pale pink rambler roses – Cornelias – buttery, faint, warm; lilac smelling of spring rain that she gave in a great swag to a teacher she loved who was in hospital, and the smell of her furs so impregnated with chypre. There was the smell of nasturtium leaves, porridge with brown sugar, and the smell of hot iron on your palm after holding on tightly at the top of the helter-skelter before you forced yourself to turn round and descend backwards down the shiny strip of steel, worn bright by the hundreds of childish bottoms who had polished it coming down for the past twenty years.

They were not exactly memories, rather the replay of sensation. Sometimes you could bring about old feelings by deliberately smelling something – the gardenia perfume that the teacher had worn for example – velvety, semi-sweet, yet with an undertone of an almost cloying peppery passion.

Words do not exist for all these original smells, only for the effect they have upon the one with the nose. They are essences that for once do not really need words, and that is comforting, resembling other timeless moments that will not disappear when Jill is older, but will return on country walks, and in Victorian suburbs, so long as the place has some history.

Jill savours these experiences and those that come fortuitously through art, and music, and love, and walking alone. They are part of the Trinity she worships, and are prolonged into late adolescence, when she is already preserving future memories, consciously remembering days and colours, intimations and conversations. She will carry away memories of love from her turbulent youth that are never to leave her, but by the time she is seventeen, fantasies of future love, and reading of love's possibilities do not occupy quite all her days.

Love remains, yet it is not fantasy that attends the Snow, but Imagination...

There are books, there are poems, there are paintings; there is language, there is music, there is knowledge: there is all the world waiting.

*

'Snow is Likely over Northern Hills...'

The snow had come, lightly,
But sinking deep
Over the Wynteredge fields,
Piled on dry-stone walls,
Slurring into the cloughs.

Those days, long ago:
That snow, lit rose at sunset,
Or sepia on the roads,
Made the silence of the rooms
Into cells padded against the world.
The hearth leapt orange,
And windows left uncurtained
At dusk let the snow hold us
In an eternal Advent.

I did not know then, as I searched
For a lost passion I had stored
Against all winters,
That winter would return
For ever in this way
Whenever the snow light was on the walls

And that the passion would be for that.

*

That day of a cold blue winter, it all suddenly came together in her mind, pointed to future states and remained for ever as a seal upon them and upon her life.

She had left the house in the morning, a house still lit up before enough light seeped into the rooms from the short day's sun. All night it had snowed and the Christmas tree stood looking out at the back garden, awaiting its turn. The snow would later drift to a great height, but for the present, as she walked out, it was frosty and the sky was beginning to clear in the east over Owram Hill.

Jill was burdened with a large post-bag, for she was temporary postman for a week. What a relief to escape from all the clashing worlds of reading where each truth seemed to cancel out another, out to the pure cold air of winter, an accredited person, walking towards an accredited job.

She greeted the wall-eyed senior postman whose walk she was helping with, and he helped her pack her bag tightly with twine-twisted bundles of letters (mostly Christmas cards). They were standing in the back room of the sub-post office along with half a dozen other sixth-formers, mostly boys. Ted, 'her' postman, was tickled that a girl should be helping him do his work, a girl to whom he had formerly delivered letters when he was on his South walk.

Jill's walk that morning, in the first fall of snow, was north of the neighbouring village, to Wynteredge. The snow was still manageable, though it was thick on the fields. If it fell again it would soon make walking clogged and difficult. But this morning was attended by the strange first quiet of snow, pink, blue and gold in this early and fugitive sun, not yet sepia from trudging feet.

There had been few cars out; not that many were found on the main road after about nine o'clock. The village and the road above it, which narrowed to a lane beyond the furthest bus-stop, the buses turning left to follow the old Turnpike road, seemed havens of solitude and peace. The few householders she saw as she moved along a row of old cottages and then up to the farms, were pleased to see her, and smiled. Some of them tipped her at the end of the week, money which she took to Ted, though he insisted on sharing it. The postmen were all pleasant, contented, men who liked walking, were happy to be alone with their thoughts, and could be trusted. She had never been so well treated. To be paid for doing a job she loved! The blood glowed under her skin and tingled in her feet. She was warm from the exercise, though the wind on the top was icy. Down the hill, then past the mullioned farm, set so lonely on the edge, past field after field of sparkling tablecloth white, edged with the black line of the dry-stone walls of millstone grit, like mourning cards. Her walk skirted the village and came back up to the Holm Garth road, across it and down again by the Stray, stopping at many detached houses, then the shops and the official return home.

There were other walks she took later, but this one was remembered. The world was muffled by a soft pedal, faces shone through here and there, and heavy envelopes bore the greetings of myriad lives. She was not tired, though she had already walked three miles with a heavy bag – and tramped back to the post office for a second bagful. There was nothing much left so she was allowed to go home for a bite of dinner and then return in the afternoon. The lads were of course in the vans which meant they got paid more for heaving parcels about.

For about twenty minutes the sun had sparkled out over the snow and the children were flailing their sledges down the park slope. But it was becoming colder and once the sun had got behind a goose-grey sky it might not come back, except at sunset. It was a wonderfully clear and dazzling light as she walked home, only becoming hushed and expectant when the sun disappeared again.

Mother had left some stew to warm up, and apple pie which Jill prepared for her father and herself in the kitchen. The back garden through the window was all white, and drifts had piled up in the night against the coal bunker, for the wind chased everything behind their house as it stood at the end of the loop of the Avenue.

The dining-room fire was banked up with slack and more coal would be put on it at tea-time. It was cosy, and she longed to bring the armchair up to the fireplace and read in the shadows.

'I'd better be off,' she said. 'I've to do the Lower Road walk this afternoon, I think, to help the other postman. I hope it won't snow again till I get back.'

She was lucky – the postmen were well on with their deliveries with all the additional help they were having, and she only had to do the houses near the Stray again, which she loved. There were Christmas trees in most of the windows and from one house she heard the sound of a piano and a children's party. She pondered the writing on the envelopes she was posting: an educated Gothic script went into the letterbox at the Helliwell's house, one of three of late eighteenth-century stone with white sills and large, long, windows and a cobbled courtyard, hidden behind the snicket. She liked to think of all the friends from unknown worlds who wrote at Christmas and penetrated the lives, unknown to her, of the various professional families who lived in the village. They were not always the richest, as far as money went, for the rich in this part of the country kept to nineteenth-century habits of thrift, were often eccentric and rented gloomy old houses, surprising all and sundry when their wills were read out. But she did not want to think of these vulgar material details, preferred to elevate her thoughts, shining and silver, feel the mystery of other lives at this time and this place, behind the lighted windows.

Suddenly, just before dusk, she was visited by a sensation of stopped time.

The roads would be for ever sheeted with snow, the children for ever faintly shouting on the hill, the lights for ever burning, the sun for ever just about to set. It was not just a mood or state of mind enhanced by the satisfaction of a well-spent day, but seemed to connect with the past lives of the village and the lanes and farms as though the past were the present and the present the past and there was no need of a future. She loved the names of places in the neighbourhood: Laverock Lane, Finkil, Ganny Hall, Slead Syke, Bonegate, Southowram and Northowram, Smithy Carr Lane, Grassy Lane, Gipsy Lane, Stoney Lane, The Coach Road, Lidgett House, Rookes Hall and Upper Rookes Hall, Shirley Manor, Bottom Hall, Till Carr Lane, Lower Wynteredge Farm and Wynteredge Hall, Shelf, Sun Woods, Judy Woods, Royds Hall, Low Moor, Denholmegate Road, Spout House Lane, Hellewell Syke, Priestley Green, Norwood Green...

As temporary postwoman, she felt she was accepted as part of the place, and she savoured the new sensation, positively welcoming the trudging round. If only the sun would always be like this, behind the elms, rooks cawing; if only this two or three square miles were all there was of the world. She felt the absolute security of home and yet, even as she did, knew that books and ideas were beckoning to her, that this afternoon – and late afternoon was her favourite time of the day – would become only another afternoon, bearing her whether she wanted or not, towards a future when this beauty, the snow, the past years would become irrevocably a Memory.

The spirit of the place sustained her, and the peaceful, bounded activity: the portrait her sister had painted of her, the library books waiting by the fire, the parents busy and self-contained, the maroon single-decker bus breasting the hill, the town with its covered market hidden in the smoky valley and the rank upon rank of hills stretching into moorland before darkness fell.

For once the Actual seemed to become the Ideal. She wanted it immutable, herself not to change, wanted the crystal gas lamps to shine in necklaces of light seen from the bedroom window purling over valleys and hills in the sharp cold air to the next village on the hill with its church and houses.

She was full of love of this place and of this time, full of anguished delight for the view that would open out from the train – as it came from the larger town over the viaduct – a view of splendid high ridges topped each by its church with rolling fields and trees and sometimes a glimpse of barer moor land. The delight always aroused in her by Christmas card snowy villages, lanterns and candlelight was the same delight she recognised in the real place. Even the sound of the town brass band playing 'Christians Awake' on Christmas morning was part of it. She was near enough to her beginnings to half-believe nothing would ever change, but far enough from them to be conscious already of a nostalgic happiness.

The feelings aroused in her by this sense of oneness with a whole, each time wrapping itself around the kernel of the first time they were felt, feelings which were already half memories, added an extra dimension to the states of mind aroused in her by art. They were not precisely the same feelings but they shared certain elements: a certain mystery, depth, and intimation of otherness. Her responses were aroused by both life and novels, poems, pieces of music, paintings. It was the 'not quite understanding', the resonances, the feeling of something lying under covers, and also the sensation of variety, of *nimiety* – of there being too much to understand, as in a piece of writing she would feel partly envious – maybe unable to grasp the depth and knowledge and experience – of that mysterious 'something' that spoke through the writer. She too was part of this inexhaustible 'given'.

She forgets for a time the books with too many disparate 'truths' or ways of looking at the world, forgets her confusion, feels only exalted. It is better to be rinsed clean of all but the pure self, striding in the sparkling snow! Yet the experience brings with it feelings similar to those rising mistily from books. The reality of the place and people pleases her, but her imagination makes it shimmer, full of unspoken truths – relationships, memories, quirks. Her timeless homecoming partakes of the eternal. Though that time, that place, are never to be repeated, and will slide away into memory, they are also fixed for ever: the book will always be waiting by the fire, the fire will always send shadows dancing on the dining-room walls, the snow will always lie hushed, the wind wuther in the chimneys and the girl lay her head down on the pillow in full expectation of happiness.

Her future dreams will be of childhood fears as well as of love and remembrance: nightmares of loss, of trying to sew tiny stitches on unbleached linen, of trying to swim...of the Pig who might return, glaring and bristling, his body sectioned like the schematic 'joints of pork' in a cookery book, sometimes to change into a grunting, sweating Bad Man chasing her. In other dreams though, beloved grandparents will never grow old and die; happiness will still be the taste of yellow Kali, the scent of Aunt Jenny's dough rising in the hearth on Thursdays, and the faint buttery scent of Father's roses.

The place will feed her for years after she has torn herself away from it.

She thought it was over, finished, just a place in which to be a child. But it slowly reasserted itself, became more real than the real place, so that whenever she returned she saw it just as it had been, heard children singing 'Now the day is over', saw the flowers, the fields, brooks, which, stopped in time, awaited resurrection through the power of Memory and Imagination.

EPILOGUE

1980

Death has already brought its horror.

Funerals are not fictions although they are the hardest ceremony to believe in. Who truly believes that a person lies in that coffin? Even, what was once a person? Even, if a whole family gathers together – the only time they may gather now.

Funerals have not changed, nor their incidence, but cemeteries are not what they were.

Other funerals were happening in this cemetery all the time she was a child, thinks Jill, but now there seem to be more of them each year. Once, she looked for births emblazoned in newspapers, now she finds names more familiar to her in the death columns.

A world separates the child Jill from the adult; more than a world separates Jill from her father and Aunt May now that they have both disappeared in coffins between the sinisterly opening doors of the crematorium.

Jill was not present the day her grandfather was buried, the week before the war began. The cemetery has no connection for her with the grandfather she knew, only with an imaginary picture of a funeral and a cemetery, since she and Nancy had not been allowed to accompany the grown-ups that August afternoon. Twenty years later, her grandmother had been buried in the same place. By that time Jill was far away and had never visited her grave. But after the deaths of her father and Aunt May, she has known she must go to the older cemetery to see the family graves.

In 1896 Grandpa bought a freehold brick grave in the consecrated part of this vast private cemetery a mile or two away from Woolsford, built on a hill overlooking it, a much more impressive place than the small cemetery where Jill once lost her penny.

The deeds to Grandpa's grave said 'in perpetuity'.

A park had been fashioned around the cemetery. It must have been a pretty spot a hundred years ago, even as the first monumental masons chipped away at the honey-coloured millstone grit, the lawns were clipped and the flower beds planted. Just as in the first cemetery, there rose neat chapels in the new Gothic, one for Church folk and one for Chapel, on each side of the central path.

What funerals they must have had, with crêpe and mutes, nodding horses' plumes, sons and daughters standing respectfully round the graves!

Even when Grandpa finally came into his investment and occupied his numbered grave, one among many hundreds, the cemetery was still well kept. His own grandfather and grandmother and his parents were buried not far away, and eventually Granny joined him there. Jill pays for inscriptions to be added when Grandpa's son and daughter die, and for the grave to be kept tidy.

For years she has intended to go, but only now, some years after the last death, has she gone.

It is not plain sailing, since for three years the cemetery company has been in the hands of the receivers and has passed into limbo. But not a featureless limbo, as she is to discover when she finally arrives before the gates on an August afternoon of cool intermittent rain.

She crosses the road and enters the gates. The lodges on each side are gutted and vandalised, their neo-Gothic arches and chimneys like those of some terrible castle. Not a soul is in sight as she walks down the path to the blackened chapel ruins.

Not only is the cemetery ugly; it is terrifying. Rank upon rank, row upon row, of graves, stretch in every direction as far as the eye can see over the waving grasses. The graves and their monuments are like some monstrous Gothic horror film that suddenly blots out the rest of the daytime world.

The blackness which used to be part of the buildings in the town when she was a child, the darkness, has swept up from the industrial valley and covers the whole large cemetery in such a way that every monument, every towering angel or catafalque with pillars, is now like a monstrous bird, a giant raven. The sight of them all, silhouetted from the path against the grey gold sky is like a vast visitation of witches.

The two chapels are also gutted by vandals, stand dark, windowless, blank, covered inside in large obscene graffiti. On every side, down every path, through the massed ranks of graves, waves the thick waist-high grass; convolvulus climbs over gravestones that flounder in deep holes. Only the tallest monuments can be readily approached and those only on the edge of paths. The rest are in a sea of oblivion. Even with a map it is impossible to locate the tombstone for which she is searching.

Wading through grass, falling down, tripping up – and now eyed in the distance by a strange-looking man – she wants to give up, to run away.

All that time ago, all those years, all those miles, to come back and find the dead have returned to anonymity, visited by ghouls and fire-raisers and unimaginative perpetrators of second-hand pagan rites at dead of night...

She must believe that the souls have gone far away and left the meaningless idle bones. Otherwise it would break her heart to feel how *their* hearts would have been broken if they had known of their future neglect.

What if she had known, talking to Granny one day over

tea, how Granny would one day lie, uncared for, dead in a wilderness? How could she have borne it? Does it matter that Grandpa's and his wife's last resting place is now a deserted ruin?

Yet Granny is alive now only in her mind and in the memory of a few others' minds. Granny does not care now, that all their lives should end in this?

They will never know.

It matters only because it affects Jill's memory of them, alters the past and is a subtle insult to the importance of their lived lives.

Perhaps, though, floating far above dead matter is a lovely essence of that past, so that all can be had for ever, in perpetuity?

In perpetual feeling, part of the past, present and future. No longer tied to the circumstantial and the morbidity of death but perpetually at rest in a world where the past, all the past, is for ever laid up. She does hope so. Jill shakes her head and forbids useless tears.

March on.

1990

In the last few years hundreds of people have laboured to restore the great cemetery to its previous glory. The paths and the plots and the graves have been cleaned and tidied, the burnt out chapels demolished. A committee has been appointed to guard against vandals; the city council has been approached. Jill has had Grandpa's grave tidied and cleaned and Great Grandpa's and Great Great Grandpa's replanted.

There they all lie again as they did before, this time in sunshine, a part now of 'Our Heritage'.

In Perpetuity

Suffer Us to Remember

All children know a smuggler's cave,
Wide sands and azure sea,
For all pale brats of Pimlico
The operative word is 'three'.

Buried in these sands and coves
Spellbound in magic rings
Sailing on, we built and saved
The gladness of imagined things.
We only knew the terror dark
That lurked in woods and fields,
We never saw the human mask wrenched off.
The grin that yields
Strange lands of fear and sickly force,
The power behind the horse.

Since then for many years we've known
What visions did not tell,
The violence of mind and bone
The sad drought of the wishing well.

O may our loves stay child's loves long
Our fears be in the mind
Allow us to recall our world
Of skies and boats and wind.
Suffer us to see the years
As bright strands on a chain
That does not weal
Close-worked with star and sheaf.
Let snow and primrose, lake, red leaf
As one they were be born again

O suffer us to remember!